Our Epidemic of Loneliness and Isolation

2023

The U.S. Surgeon General's Advisory on the Healing Effects of Social Connection and Community

Table of Contents

Letter from the Surgeon General

Dr. Vivek H. Murthy
19th and 21st Surgeon General
of the United States

When I first took office as Surgeon General in 2014, I didn't view loneliness as a public health concern. But that was before I embarked on a cross-country listening tour, where I heard stories from my fellow Americans that surprised me.

People began to tell me they felt isolated, invisible, and insignificant. Even when they couldn't put their finger on the word "lonely," time and time again, people of all ages and socioeconomic backgrounds, from every corner of the country, would tell me, "I have to shoulder all of life's burdens by myself," or "if I disappear tomorrow, no one will even notice."

It was a lightbulb moment for me: social disconnection was far more common than I had realized.

In the scientific literature, I found confirmation of what I was hearing. In recent years, about one-in-two adults in America reported experiencing loneliness.[1-3] And that was before the COVID-19 pandemic cut off so many of us from friends, loved ones, and support systems, exacerbating loneliness and isolation.

Loneliness is far more than just a bad feeling—it harms both individual and societal health. It is associated with a greater risk of cardiovascular disease, dementia, stroke, depression, anxiety, and premature death. The mortality impact of being socially disconnected is similar to that caused by smoking up to 15 cigarettes a day,[4] and even greater than that associated with obesity and physical inactivity. And the harmful consequences of a society that lacks social connection can be felt in our schools, workplaces, and civic organizations, where performance, productivity, and engagement are diminished.

Given the profound consequences of loneliness and isolation, we have an opportunity, and an obligation, to make the same investments in addressing social connection that we have made in addressing tobacco use, obesity, and the addiction crisis. This Surgeon General's Advisory shows us how to build more connected lives and a more connected society.

If we fail to do so, we will pay an ever-increasing price in the form of our individual and collective health and well-being. And we will continue to splinter and divide until we can no longer stand as a community or a country. Instead of coming together to take on the great challenges before us, we will further retreat to our corners—angry, sick, and alone.

We are called to build a movement to mend the social fabric of our nation. It will take all of us—individuals and families, schools and workplaces, health care and public health systems, technology companies, governments, faith organizations, and communities—working together to destigmatize loneliness and change our cultural and policy response to it. It will require reimagining the structures, policies, and programs that shape a community to best support the development of healthy relationships.

Each of us can start now, in our own lives, by strengthening our connections and relationships. Our individual relationships are an untapped resource—a source of healing hiding in plain sight. They can help us live healthier, more productive, and more fulfilled lives. Answer that phone call from a friend. Make time to share a meal. Listen without the distraction of your phone. Perform an act of service. Express yourself authentically. The keys to human connection are simple, but extraordinarily powerful.

> Each of us can start now, in our own lives, by strengthening our connections and relationships.

Loneliness and isolation represent profound threats to our health and well-being. But we have the power to respond. By taking small steps every day to strengthen our relationships, and by supporting community efforts to rebuild social connection, we can rise to meet this moment together. We can build lives and communities that are healthier and happier. And we can ensure our country and the world are better poised than ever to take on the challenges that lay ahead.

Our future depends on what we do today.

Vivek Murthy

Vivek H. Murthy, M.D., M.B.A.
19th and 21st Surgeon General of the United States
Vice Admiral, United States Public Health Service

Our Epidemic of Loneliness and Isolation: The U.S. Surgeon General's Advisory on the Healing Effects of Social Connection and Community

5

About the Advisory

LEARN MORE

Visit our website for more information and resources about social connection: **SurgeonGeneral.gov/Connection**

A Surgeon General's Advisory is a public statement that calls the American people's attention to an urgent public health issue and provides recommendations for how it should be addressed. Advisories are reserved for significant public health challenges that require the nation's immediate awareness and action.

This advisory calls attention to the importance of social connection for individual health as well as on community-wide metrics of health and well-being, and conversely the significant consequences when social connection is lacking. While social connection is often considered an individual challenge, this advisory explores and explains the cultural, community, and societal dynamics that drive connection and disconnection. It also offers recommendations for increasing and strengthening social connection through a whole-of-society approach. The advisory presents a framework for a national strategy with specific recommendations for the institutions that shape our day-to-day lives: governments, health care systems and insurers, public health departments, research institutions, philanthropy, schools, workplaces, community-based organizations, technology companies, and the media.

This advisory draws upon decades of research from the scientific disciplines of sociology, psychology, neuroscience, political science, economics, and public health, among others. This document is not an exhaustive review of the literature. Rather, the advisory was developed through a substantial review of the available evidence, primarily found via electronic searches of research articles published in English and resources suggested by a wide range of subject matter experts, with priority given to meta-analyses and systematic literature reviews. The recommendations in the advisory draw upon the scientific literature and previously published recommendations from the National Academies of Sciences, Engineering and Medicine, the Centers for Disease Control and Prevention, the American Heart Association, and the World Health Organization.

The findings and recommendations in the advisory are also informed by consultations with subject matter experts from academia, health care, education, government, and other sectors of society, including more than 50 identified experts who reviewed and provided individual detailed feedback on an early draft that has informed this advisory.

For additional background and to read other Surgeon General's Advisories, visit **SurgeonGeneral.gov**

Our Epidemic of Loneliness and Isolation: The U.S. Surgeon General's Advisory on the Healing Effects of Social Connection and Community

6

Glossary

Belonging
A fundamental human need — the feeling of deep connection with social groups, physical places, and individual and collective experiences.[5]

Collective Efficacy
The willingness of community members to act on behalf of the common good of the group or community.[6]

Empathy
The capability to understand and feel the emotional states of others, resulting in compassionate behavior.[7,8]

Loneliness
A subjective distressing experience that results from perceived isolation or inadequate meaningful connections, where inadequate refers to the discrepancy or unmet need between an individual's preferred and actual experience.[9,10]

Norms of Reciprocity
A sense of reciprocal obligation that is not only a transactional mutual benefit but a generalized one; by treating others well, we anticipate that we will also be treated well.[11,12]

Social Capital
The resources to which individuals and groups have access through their social connections.[13,14] The term social capital is often used as an umbrella for both social support and social cohesion.[15]

Social Cohesion
The sense of solidarity within groups, marked by strong social connections and high levels of social participation, that generates trust, norms of reciprocity, and a sense of belonging.[13,15-18]

Social Connectedness
The degree to which any individual or population might fall along the continuum of achieving social connection needs.[19]

Social Connection
A continuum of the size and diversity of one's social network and roles, the functions these relationships serve, and their positive or negative qualities.[10,19,20]

Social Disconnection
Objective or subjective deficits in social connection, including deficits in relationships and roles, their functions, and/or quality.[19]

Social Infrastructure
The programs (such as volunteer organizations, sports groups, religious groups, and member associations), policies (like public transportation, housing, and education), and physical elements of a community (such as libraries, parks, green spaces, and playgrounds) that support the development of social connection.

Social Isolation
Objectively having few social relationships, social roles, group memberships, and infrequent social interaction.[19,21]

Social Negativity
The presence of harmful interactions or relationships, rather than the absence of desired social interactions or relationships.[19,22]

Social Networks
The individuals and groups a person is connected to and the interconnections among relationships. These "webs of social connections" provide the structure for various social connection functions to potentially operate.[18,23]

Social Norms
The unwritten rules that we follow that serve as a social contract to provide order and predictability in society. The social groups we belong to provide information and expectations, and constraints on what is acceptable and appropriate behavior.[24] Social norms reinforce or discourage health-related and risky behaviors (lifestyle factors, vaccination, substance use, etc.).[25]

Social Participation
A person's involvement in activities in the community or society that provides interaction with others.[26,27]

Social Support
The perceived or actual availability of informational, tangible, and emotional resources from others, commonly one's social network.[10,28]

Solitude
A state of aloneness by choice that does not involve feeling lonely.

Trust
An individual's expectation of positive intent and benevolence from the actions of other people and groups.[29-31]

Chapter 1

Overview

Introduction: Why Social Connection Matters

Our relationships and interactions with family, friends, colleagues, and neighbors are just some of what create social connection. Our connection with others and our community is also informed by our neighborhoods, digital environments, schools, and workplaces. Social connection— the structure, function, and quality of our relationships with others—is a critical and underappreciated contributor to individual and population health, community safety, resilience, and prosperity.[6,17,32-36] However, far too many Americans lack social connection in one or more ways, compromising these benefits and leading to poor health and other negative outcomes.

People may lack social connection in a variety of ways, though it is often illustrated in scientific research by measuring loneliness and social isolation. Social isolation and loneliness are related, but they are not the same. Social isolation is objectively having few social relationships, social roles, group memberships, and infrequent social interaction.[19,21] On the other hand, loneliness is a subjective internal state. It's the distressing experience that results from perceived isolation or unmet need between an individual's preferred and actual experience.[9,10,19]

The lack of social connection poses a significant risk for individual health and longevity. Loneliness and social isolation increase the risk for premature death by 26% and 29% respectively.[37] More broadly, lacking social connection can increase the risk for premature death as much as smoking up to 15 cigarettes a day.[4] In addition, poor or insufficient social connection is associated with increased risk of disease, including a 29% increased risk of heart disease and a 32% increased risk of stroke.[38] Furthermore, it is associated with increased risk for anxiety, depression,[39] and dementia.[40,41] Additionally, the lack of social connection may increase susceptibility to viruses and respiratory illness.[42]

KEY DATA

Lacking social connection can increase the risk for premature death as much as smoking up to 15 cigarettes a day.

Our Epidemic of Loneliness and Isolation: The U.S. Surgeon General's Advisory on the Healing Effects of Social Connection and Community

8

The lack of social connection can have significant economic costs to individuals, communities, and society. Social isolation among older adults alone accounts for an estimated $6.7 billion in excess Medicare spending annually, largely due to increased hospital and nursing facility spending.[43] Moreover, beyond direct health care spending, loneliness and isolation are associated with lower academic achievement[44,45] and worse performance at work.[46-48] In the U.S., stress-related absenteeism attributed to loneliness costs employers an estimated $154 billion annually.[46] The impact of social connection not only affects individuals, but also the communities they live in. Social connection is an important social determinant of health, and more broadly, of community well-being, including (but not limited to) population health, community resilience when natural hazards strike, community safety, economic prosperity, and representative government.[13,15,17,34-36,49,50]

What drives these profound health and well-being outcomes? Social connection is a fundamental human need, as essential to survival as food, water, and shelter. Throughout history, our ability to rely on one another has been crucial to survival. Now, even in modern times, we human beings are biologically wired for social connection. Our brains have adapted to expect proximity to others.[51,52] Our distant ancestors relied on others to help them meet their basic needs. Living in isolation, or outside the group, means having to fulfill the many difficult demands of survival on one's own. This requires far more effort and reduces one's chances of survival.[52] Despite current advancements that now allow us to live without engaging with others (e.g., food delivery, automation, remote entertainment), our biological need to connect remains.

KEY DATA

Approximately half of U.S. adults report experiencing loneliness, with some of the highest rates among young adults.

The health and societal impacts of social isolation and loneliness are a critical public health concern in light of mounting evidence that millions of Americans lack adequate social connection in one or more ways. A 2022 study found that when people were asked how close they felt to others emotionally, only 39% of adults in the U.S. said that they felt very connected to others.[53] An important indicator of this declining social connection is an increase in the proportion of Americans experiencing loneliness. Recent surveys have found that approximately half of U.S. adults report experiencing loneliness, with some of the highest rates among young adults.[1-3] These estimates and multiple other studies indicate that loneliness and isolation are more widespread than many of the other major health issues of our day, including smoking (12.5% of U.S. adults),[54] diabetes (14.7%),[55] and obesity (41.9%),[56] and with comparable levels of risk to health and premature death. Despite such high prevalence, less than 20% of individuals who often or always feel lonely or isolated recognize it as a major problem.[57]

Our Epidemic of Loneliness and Isolation: The U.S. Surgeon General's Advisory on the Healing Effects of Social Connection and Community

9

Together, this represents an urgent public health concern. Every level of increase in social connection corresponds with a risk reduction across many health conditions. Further, social connection can be a proactive approach to living a fulfilled and happy life, enhancing life satisfaction, educational attainment, and performance in the workplace, as well as contributing to more-connected communities that are healthier, safer, and more prosperous.

Unsurprisingly, social connection is generally not something we can do alone and not something that is accessible equitably. That is partially because we need others to connect with, but also because our society—including our schools, workplaces, neighborhoods, public policies, and digital environments—plays a role in either facilitating or hindering social connection.[10,32] Moreover, it is critical to carefully consider equity in any approach to addressing social connection, as access and barriers to social opportunities are often not the same for everyone and often reinforce longstanding and historical inequities.

This advisory calls attention to the critical role that social connection plays in individual and societal health and well-being and offers a framework for how we can all contribute to advancing social connection.

What is Social Connection?

Social connection can encompass the interactions, relationships, roles, and sense of connection individuals, communities, or society may experience.[10,19,20] An individual's level of social connection is not simply determined by the number of close relationships they have. There are many ways we can connect socially, and many ways we can lack social connection. These generally fall under one of three vital components of social connection: structure, function, and quality.

- **Structure**
  The number of relationships, variety of relationships (e.g., co-worker, friend, family, neighbor), and the frequency of interactions with others.

- **Function**
  The degree to which others can be relied upon for various needs.

- **Quality**
  The degree to which relationships and interactions with others are positive, helpful, or satisfying (vs. negative, unhelpful, or unsatisfying).

These three vital components of social connection are each important for health,[4,32] and may influence health in different ways.[20]

The Three Vital Components of
Social Connection

The extent to which an individual is socially connected depends on multiple factors, including:

Structure

The number and variety of relationships and frequency of interactions

Function

The degree to which relationships serve various needs

Quality

The positive and negative aspects of relationships and interactions

EXAMPLES

Household size

Friend circle size

Marital/partnership status

EXAMPLES

Emotional support

Mentorship

Support in a crisis

EXAMPLES

Relationship satisfaction

Relationship strain

Social inclusion or exclusion

Source: Holt-Lunstad J. Why Social Relationships Are Important for Physical Health: A Systems Approach to Understanding and Modifying Risk and Protection. *Annu Rev Psychol.* 2018;69:437-458.

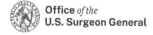
Office *of the*
U.S. Surgeon General

FIGURE 1: The Three Vital Components of Social Connection

It's also critical to understand other defining features of social connection.

First, it is a continuum. Too often, indicators of social connection or social disconnection are considered in dichotomous ways (e.g., someone is lonely or they're not), but the evidence points more to a gradient.[58,59] Everyone falls somewhere on the continuum of social connection, with low social connection generally associated with poorer outcomes and higher social connection with better outcomes.[59]

Second, social connection is dynamic. The amount and quality of social connection in our lives is not static. Social connectedness changes over time and can be improved or compromised for a myriad of reasons. Illness, moves, job transitions, and countless other life events, as well as changes in one's community and society, can all impact social connectedness in one direction or another. Further, how long we remain on one end of the continuum may matter. Transient feelings of loneliness may be less problematic, or even adaptive, because the distressing feeling motivates us to reconnect socially.[60] Similarly, temporary experiences of solitude may help us manage social demands.[61] However, chronic loneliness (even if someone is not isolated) and isolation (even if someone is not lonely) represent a significant health concern.[21,62,63]

Third, much like the absence of disease does not equate to good health, the absence of social deficits (e.g., loneliness) does not necessarily equate to high levels of social connection. Although some measures of social connection represent the full continuum, others only focus on deficits, which do not capture the degree to which social assets may contribute to resilience, or even enable thriving.[58] Consider two examples: first, an individual who is part of a large, highly-involved family, and second, an individual who has regular contact with colleagues through work but has little time for personal relationships outside of work. In each case, such an individual is not objectively isolated and may not feel subjectively lonely. However, in both cases key measures of isolation and loneliness may miss whether they are reaping the benefits of social connection in other ways, such as feeling adequately supported or having high-quality, close relationships.

Current Trends: Is Social Connection Declining?

Across many measures, Americans appear to be becoming less socially connected over time.[12,64] This is not a new problem—certain declines have been occurring for decades. While precise estimates of the rates of social connection nationally can be challenging because studies vary based on which indicator is measured, when the same measure is used at multiple time points, we can identify trends.

Our Epidemic of Loneliness and Isolation: The U.S. Surgeon General's Advisory on the Healing Effects of Social Connection and Community

12

Changes in key indicators, including individual social participation, demographics, community involvement, and use of technology over time, suggest both overall societal declines in social connection and that, currently, a significant portion of Americans lack adequate social connection.

A fraying of the social fabric can also be seen more broadly in society. Trust in each other and major institutions is at near historic lows.[65] Polls conducted in 1972 showed that roughly 45% of Americans felt they could reliably trust other Americans; however, that proportion shrank to roughly 30% in 2016.[66] This corresponds with levels of polarization being at near historic highs.[65,67] These phenomena combine to have widespread effects on society, including many of the most pressing issues we face as a nation.

KEY DATA

Polls conducted in 1972 showed that roughly 45% of Americans felt they could reliably trust other Americans; however, that proportion shrank to roughly 30% in 2016.

Trends in Social Networks and Social Participation

Social networks are getting smaller, and levels of social participation are declining distinct from whether individuals report that they are lonely. For example, objective measures of social exposure obtained from 2003-2020 find that social isolation, measured by the average time spent alone, increased from 2003 (285-minutes/day, 142.5-hours/month) to 2019 (309-minutes/day, 154.5-hours/month) and continued to increase in 2020 (333-minutes/day, 166.5-hours/month).[64] This represents an increase of 24 hours per month spent alone. At the same time, social participation across several types of relationships has steadily declined. For instance, the amount of time respondents engaged with friends socially in-person decreased from 2003 (60-minutes/day, 30-hours/month) to 2020 (20-minutes/day, 10-hours/month).[64] This represents a decrease of 20 hours per month spent engaging with friends. This decline is starkest for young people ages 15 to 24. For this age group, time spent in-person with friends has reduced by nearly 70% over almost two decades, from roughly 150 minutes per day in 2003 to 40 minutes per day in 2020.[64] The COVID-19 pandemic accelerated trends in declining social participation.

The number of close friendships has also declined over several decades. Among people not reporting loneliness or social isolation, nearly 90% have three or more confidants.[57] Yet, almost half of Americans (49%) in 2021 reported having three or fewer close friends—only about a quarter (27%) reported the same in 1990.[68] Social connection continued to decline during the COVID-19 pandemic, with one study finding a 16% decrease in network size from June 2019 to June 2020 among participants.[69]

Our Epidemic of Loneliness and Isolation: The U.S. Surgeon General's Advisory on the Healing Effects of Social Connection and Community

13

National Trends for
Social Connection

From 2003 to 2020, time spent alone increased, while time spent on in-person social engagement decreased.

ANNUAL DAILY AVERAGE IN MINUTES

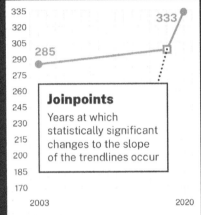

Joinpoints

Years at which statistically significant changes to the slope of the trendlines occur

Social Isolation

an increase of
24 hours per month

Household Family Social Engagement

a decrease of
5 hours per month

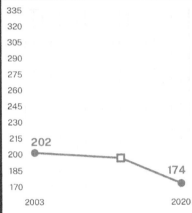

Companionship

a decrease of
14 hours per month

Companionship refers to shared leisure for the sake of enjoyment and intrinsic satisfaction

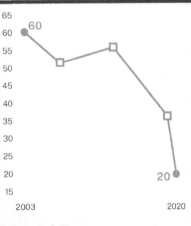

Social Engagement with Friends

a decrease of
20 hours per month

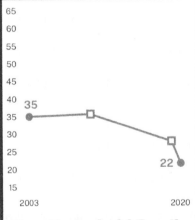

Non-Household Family Social Engagement

a decrease of
6.5 hours per month

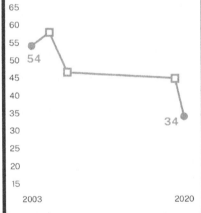

Social Engagement with Others

a decrease of
10 hours per month

YEAR

Source: Adapted from Viji Diane Kannan, Peter J. Veazie, US Trends in Social Isolation, Social Engagement, and Companionship: Nationally and by Age, Sex, Race/ethnicity, Family Income, and Work Hours, 2003–2020, *SSM - Population Health*, Volume 21, 2023. The joinpoints are visual approximations.

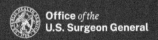

Office *of the*
U.S. Surgeon General

FIGURE 2: National Trends for Social Connection

Our Epidemic of Loneliness and Isolation: The U.S. Surgeon General's Advisory on the Healing Effects of Social Connection and Community

14

Demographic Trends

Societal trends, including demographic changes such as age, marital/partnership status, and household size, also provide clues to current trends. For example, family size and marriage rates have been in steady decline for decades.[70] The percentage of Americans living alone has also increased decade-to-decade. In 1960, single-person households accounted for only 13% of all U.S. households.[70] In 2022, that number more than doubled, to 29% of all households.[70]

The reasons people choose to remain single or unmarried, have smaller families, and live alone over time are complex and encompass many factors. Yet at the same time, it is important to acknowledge the contribution these demographic changes have on social disconnection because of the significant health impacts identified in the scientific evidence. Moreover, awareness can help individuals consider these impacts and cultivate ways to foster sufficient social connection outside of chosen traditional means and structures.

> Awareness can help individuals consider these impacts and cultivate ways to foster sufficient social connection outside of chosen traditional means and structures.

The research in this section points to overall declines in some of the critical structural elements of social connection (e.g., marital status, household size), which helps to explain increases in reported loneliness and social isolation and contributes to the overall crisis of connection we are experiencing. Finally, this suggests we have fewer informal supports to draw upon in times of need—all while the number of older individuals and those living with chronic conditions continues to increase.

Trends in Community Involvement

Although the concept of community has evolved over time, many traditional indicators of community involvement, including with religious groups, clubs, and labor unions, show declining trends in the United States since at least the 1970s.[12,71] In 2018, only 16% of Americans reported that they felt very attached to their local community.[72]

KEY DATA

16%

In 2018, only 16% of Americans reported that they felt very attached to their local community.

Membership in organizations that have been important pillars of community connection have declined significantly in this time. Take faith organizations, for example. Research produced by Gallup, Pew Research Center, and the National Opinion Research Center's General Social Survey demonstrates that since the 1970s, religious preference, affiliation, and participation among U.S. adults have declined.[73-75] In 2020, only 47% of Americans said they belonged to a church, synagogue, or mosque. This is down from 70% in 1999 and represents a dip below 50% for the first time in the history of the survey question.[75] Religious or faith-based groups can be a source for regular social contact, serve as a community of support, provide meaning and purpose, create a sense of belonging around shared values and beliefs, and are associated with reduced risk-taking behaviors.[76-78] As a consequence of this decline in participation, individuals' health may be undermined in different ways.[16]

What Leads Us to Be More or Less Socially Connected?

A wide variety of factors can influence an individual or community's level of social connection. One organizing tool that helps us better understand these factors is the social-ecological model.[79,80] This model organizes the interrelated factors that affect health on the individual level, in our relationships, in our communities, and in society. Each of these levels—from the smallest to the broadest—contribute to social connection and its associated risks and protection for health.

Our Epidemic of Loneliness and Isolation: The U.S. Surgeon General's Advisory on the Healing Effects of Social Connection and Community

16

Factors That Can Shape Social Connection

Individual
- Chronic disease
- Sensory and functional impairments
- Mental health
- Physical health
- Personality
- Race
- Gender
- Socioeconomic status
- Life stage

Relationships
- Structure, function, and quality
- Household size
- Characteristics and behaviors of others
- Empathy

Community
- Outdoor space
- Housing
- Schools
- Workplace
- Local government
- Local business
- Community organizations
- Health care
- Transportation

Society
- Norms and values
- Public policies
- Tech environment and use
- Civic engagement
- Democratic norms
- Historical inequities

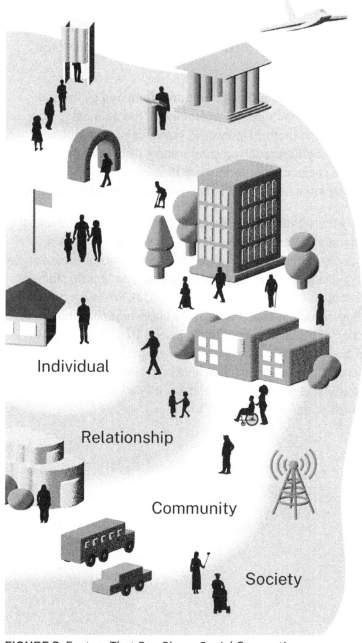

Office *of the* U.S. Surgeon General

FIGURE 3: Factors That Can Shape Social Connection

Our Epidemic of Loneliness and Isolation: The U.S. Surgeon General's Advisory on the Healing Effects of Social Connection and Community

17

Social connection is most often viewed as driven by the individual—one's genetics, health, socioeconomic status, race, gender, age, household living situation, and personality, among other factors. These can influence motivation, ability, or access to connect socially. As we've seen, the level of one's connection is also dependent on the structure, function, and quality of relationships. However, connectedness is influenced by more than simply personal or interpersonal factors. It is also shaped by the social infrastructure of the community (or communities) in which one is born, grows up, learns, plays, works, and ages.

Social infrastructure includes the physical assets of a community (such as libraries and parks), programs (such as volunteer organizations and member associations), and local policies (such as public transportation and housing) that support the development of social connection.

The social infrastructure of these communities is in turn influenced by broader social policies, cultural norms, the technology environment, the political environment, and macroeconomic factors. Moreover, individuals are simultaneously influenced by societal-level conditions such as cooperation, discrimination, inequality, and the collective social connectedness or disconnectedness of the community.[23] All of these shape the availability of opportunities for social connection.

In sum, social connection is more than a personal issue. The structural and social characteristics of the community produce the settings in which people build, maintain, and grow their social networks.[36,81,82] Because many contributors to social connection go beyond an individual's control, in order to promote health, change is needed across the full scope of the social-ecological model. While every factor listed in **Figure 3**, as well as some not captured, can be important contributors to social connection, it's important to look across these levels. That gives us clues to barriers to connection and the types of interventions which could successfully increase social connection. This broader view can also help identify what places groups at highest risk for social isolation and loneliness, as well as factors that reinforce cycles of risk or resilience.

...in order to promote health, change is needed across the full scope of the social-ecological model.

Our Epidemic of Loneliness and Isolation: The U.S. Surgeon General's Advisory on the Healing Effects of Social Connection and Community

18

Groups at Highest Risk for Social Disconnection

Anyone of any age or background can experience loneliness and isolation, but some groups are at higher risk than others. Not all individuals or groups experience the factors that facilitate or become barriers to social connection equally. Some people or groups are exposed to greater barriers. It's critical to examine and highlight the disproportionate risk they face and to target interventions to address their needs.

Although risk may differ across indicators of social disconnection, currently, studies find the highest prevalence for loneliness and isolation among people with poor physical or mental health, disabilities, financial insecurity, those who live alone, single parents, as well as younger and older populations.[1,64,83] For example, while the highest rates of social isolation are found among older adults,[64] young adults are almost twice as likely to report feeling lonely than those over 65.[1] The rate of loneliness among young adults has increased every year between 1976 and 2019.[84] In addition, lower-income adults are more likely to be lonely than those with higher incomes. Sixty-three percent of adults who earn less than $50,000 per year are considered lonely, which is 10 percentage points higher than those who earn more than $50,000 per year.[1] These data do not suggest that individual or demographic factors inherently generate loneliness or isolation. Rather, the data enable us to understand the different socioeconomic, political, and cultural mechanisms that may indicate higher risk for certain groups and lead to loneliness and isolation.

Additional at-risk groups may include individuals from ethnic and racial minority groups, LGBTQ+ individuals, rural residents, victims of domestic violence, and those who experience discrimination or marginalization. Further research is needed to fully understand the disproportionate impacts of social disconnection.

Impacts of Technology on Social Connection

There is more and more evidence pointing to the importance of our environments for health, and the same is true for digital environments and our social health. A variety of technologies have quickly and dramatically changed how we live, work, communicate, and socialize. These technologies include social media, smartphones, virtual reality, remote work, artificial intelligence, and assistive technologies, to name just a few.

These technologies are pervasive in our lives. Nearly all teens and adults under 65 (96-99%), and 75% of adults 65 and over, say that they use the internet.[85] Americans spend an average of six hours per day on digital media.[86] One-in-three U.S. adults 18 and over report that they are online "almost constantly,"[87] and

Our Epidemic of Loneliness and Isolation: The U.S. Surgeon General's Advisory on the Healing Effects of Social Connection and Community

19

the percentage of teens ages 13 to 17 years who say they are online "almost constantly" has doubled since 2015.[88] When looking at social media specifically, the percentage of U.S. adults 18 and over who reported using social media increased from 5% in 2005 to roughly 80% in 2019.[89] Among teens ages 13 to 17 years, 95% report using social media as of 2022, with more than half reporting it would be hard to give up social media.[88] Although tech adoption is relatively high among all groups, Americans with disabilities,[90] adults with lower incomes,[91] and Americans from rural areas[92] continue to experience a persistent, albeit shrinking, digital divide. They are relatively less likely to own a computer, smartphone, or tablet, or have broadband internet access.[90-92]

Technology has evolved rapidly, and the evidence around its impact on our relationships has been complex. Each type of technology, the way in which it is used, and the characteristics of who is using it, needs to be considered when determining how it may contribute to greater or reduced risk for social disconnection. There are multiple meta-analyses[93-96] and reviews[97-105] examining this topic that identify both benefits and harms.

KEY DATA

In a U.S.-based study, participants who reported using social media for more than two hours a day had about double the odds of reporting increased perceptions of social isolation compared to those who used social media for less than 30 minutes per day.

Several examples of benefits include technology that can foster connection by providing opportunities to stay in touch with friends and family, offering other routes for social participation for those with disabilities, and creating opportunities to find community, especially for those from marginalized groups.[97,106-108] For example, online support groups allow individuals to share their personal experiences and to seek, receive, and provide **social support**—including information, advice, and emotional support.[95,104]

Several examples of harms include technology that displaces in-person engagement, monopolizes our attention, reduces the quality of our interactions, and even diminishes our self-esteem.[97,109,110] This can lead to greater loneliness, fear of missing out, conflict, and reduced social connection. For example, frequent phone use during face-to-face interactions between parents and children, and between family and friends, increased distraction, reduced conversation quality, and lowered self-reported enjoyment of time spent together in-person.[111-113] In a U.S.-based study, participants who reported using social media for more than two hours a day had about double the odds of reporting increased perceptions of social isolation compared to those who used social media for less than 30 minutes per day.[114] Additionally, targets of online harassment report feelings of increased loneliness, isolation, and relationship problems, as well as lower self-esteem and trust in others.[115] Evidence shows that even perpetrators of cyberbullying experience weakened emotional bonds with social contacts and deficits in perceived belongingness.[115]

Understanding how technology can enhance or detract from social connection is complicated by ever-changing social media algorithms, complex differences in individual technology use, and balancing concerns over obtaining private user data. Advancing research in this area is essential. With that said, the existing evidence illustrates that we have reason to be concerned about the impact of some kinds of technology use on our relationships, our degree of social connection, and our health.

> ...the existing evidence illustrates that we have reason to be concerned about the impact of some kinds of technology use on our relationships, our degree of social connection, and our health.

Risk and Resilience Can Be Reinforcing

The factors that facilitate, or become barriers to, social connection can also reinforce either a virtuous or vicious cycle.[116] Economic status, health, and service are just a few illustrative examples—better social connection can lead to better health, whereas less social connection can lead to poorer health. However, each of these can be reinforcing. Being in poorer health can become a barrier to engaging socially, reducing social opportunities and support, and reinforcing a vicious cycle of poorer health and less connection.[117-119] A similar kind of pattern could occur among those struggling financially. For example, financial insecurity may require someone to work multiple jobs, resulting in less leisure time and limiting opportunities for social participation and connection—which, in turn, could provide fewer resources and financial opportunities. While these cycles can be reinforcing, they are not always negative. There is, for instance, a virtuous cycle between social connection and volunteerism or service. Those who are more connected to their communities are more likely to engage in service, and those who are engaged in service are more likely to feel connected to their communities and the individuals in it.[120] Interestingly, there is also evidence showing that the well-being benefits associated with volunteering are even greater for those with higher social connectedness than those with less.[121] Because these cycles can be reinforcing, prioritizing social connection can not only disrupt vicious cycles but also reinforce virtuous ones.

Lessons from the COVID-19 Pandemic

While social connection had been declining for decades prior to the COVID-19 pandemic, the onset of the pandemic, with its lockdowns and stay-at-home orders, was a critical time during which the issue of connection came to the forefront of public consciousness, raising awareness about this critical and ongoing public health concern.

Many of us felt lonely or isolated in a way we had never experienced before. We postponed or canceled meaningful life moments and celebrations like birthdays, graduations, and marriages. Children's education shifted online—and they missed out on the many benefits of interacting with their friends. Many people lost jobs and homes. We were unable to visit our children, siblings, parents, or grandparents. Many lost loved ones. We experienced feelings of anxiety, stress, fear, sadness, grief, anger, and pain through the loss of these moments, rituals, celebrations, and relationships.

Although the COVID-19 pandemic was a collective experience, it impacted certain populations differently. Frontline workers had a different experience than those who could work from home. Parents managing their own work and their children's online school had a different experience than single young people unable to interact in-person with friends. And those at greater risk of severe COVID-19, including older individuals, those living in nursing homes, and people with underlying health conditions, faced unique challenges. Emerging data suggests that people with close and positive familial connections may have had a different experience than those without. A recent national survey showed that, by April 2021, 1 in 4 individuals reported feeling less close to family members compared to the beginning of the pandemic.[122] Yet, at the same time, about 1 in 5 said they felt closer to family members,[122] perhaps indicating that the pandemic exacerbated existing family dynamics of connection or disconnection.

We also witnessed first responders, health care workers, community members, neighbors, and volunteers stepping up and offering their social support to one another. Service can be a powerful source of connection. From September 2020 to September 2021, the majority (51%) of U.S. individuals ages 16 and older reported informally helping others.[123] This represents more than 120 million U.S. individuals helping informally, in addition to an estimated 60 million individuals formally volunteering through an organization during the same period.[123] By engaging in service work, many were able to find and create pockets of connection for themselves and others during a public health crisis.

While profoundly disruptive in so many ways, the COVID-19 pandemic offers an opportunity to reflect more deeply on the state of social connection in our lives and in society. As we emerge from this era, rebuilding social connection and community offers us a promising and hopeful way forward.

Our Epidemic of Loneliness and Isolation: The U.S. Surgeon General's Advisory on the Healing Effects of Social Connection and Community

22

Chapter 2   How Social Connection Impacts Individual Health and Well-Being

Extensive scientific findings from a variety of disciplines, including epidemiology, neuroscience, medicine, psychology, and sociology, converge on the same conclusion: social connection is a significant predictor of longevity and better physical, cognitive, and mental health, while social isolation and loneliness are significant predictors of premature death and poor health.[10,20,32,124] In fact, the benefits of social connection extend beyond health-related outcomes. They influence an individual's educational attainment, workplace satisfaction, economic prosperity, and overall feelings of well-being and life fulfillment. This chapter summarizes the rapidly growing body of evidence on the relationship between various indicators of social connection and these outcomes for individuals.

Individual Health Outcomes

Survival and Mortality

> "Over four decades of research has produced robust evidence that lacking social connection — and in particular, scoring high on measures of social isolation — is associated with a significantly increased risk for early death from all causes."[10]
>
> 2020 Consensus Study Report,
> National Academies of Sciences Engineering and Medicine

Evidence across scientific disciplines converges on the conclusion that socially connected people live longer. Large population studies have documented that, among initially healthy people tracked over time, those who are more socially connected live longer, while those who experience social deficits, including isolation, loneliness, and poor-quality relationships, are more likely to die earlier, regardless of the cause of death.[37,125-128] Systematic research demonstrating the link between social connection and mortality risk dates to one of the first large-scale longitudinal epidemiological studies conducted in 1979.[129] This research found that people who lacked social connection were more than twice as likely than those with greater social connection to die within the follow-up period, even after accounting for age, health status, socioeconomic status, and health practices.[129]

More recent estimates, based on synthesizing data across 148 studies, with an average of 7.5 years of follow-up, suggest that social connection increases the odds of survival by 50%.[128] Indeed, the effects of social connection, isolation, and loneliness on mortality are comparable, and in some cases greater, than those of many other risk factors (see **Figure 4**) including lifestyle factors (e.g., smoking, alcohol consumption, physical inactivity), traditional clinical risks factors (e.g., high blood pressure, body mass index, cholesterol levels), environmental factors (e.g., air pollution), and clinical interventions (e.g., flu vaccine, high blood pressure medication, rehabilitation).[128,130]

KEY DATA

50%

Data across 148 studies, with an average of 7.5 years of follow-up, suggest that social connection increases the odds of survival by 50%.

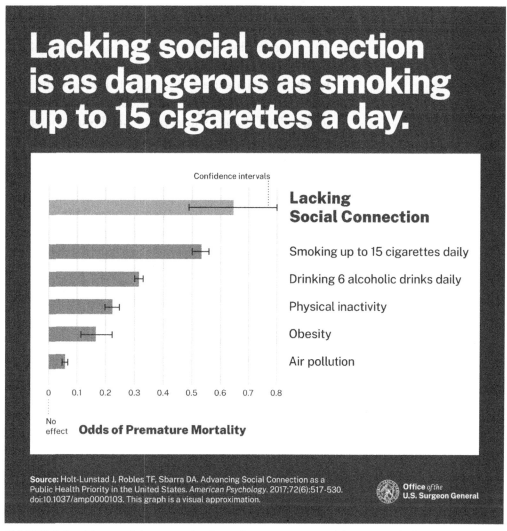

FIGURE 4: Lacking social connection is as dangerous as smoking up to 15 cigarettes a day.

Over the years, the number of studies, the rigor of their methods, and the size of the samples have all increased substantially, providing stronger confidence in this evidence. These replicate the finding that social connection decreases the risk of premature death.

Taken together, this research establishes that the lack of social connection is an independent risk factor for deaths from all causes, including deaths caused by diseases.[131]

Cardiovascular Disease

The evidence linking social connection to physical health is strongest in heart disease and stroke outcomes.[10,58] Dozens of studies have found that social isolation and loneliness significantly increase the risk of morbidities from these conditions.[10,132,133] Among this evidence, a synthesis of data across 16 independent longitudinal studies shows poor social relationships (social isolation, poor social support, loneliness) were associated with a 29% increase in the risk of heart disease and a 32% increase in the risk of stroke.[38] Interestingly, these effects can begin early in life and stretch over a lifetime. Research has also found that childhood social isolation is associated with increased cardiovascular risk factors such as obesity, high blood pressure, and blood glucose levels in adulthood.[133-135] Further, in a 2022 statement, the American Heart Association concluded that "social isolation and loneliness are common, yet underrecognized, determinants of cardiovascular health and brain health."[133]

Heart failure patients who reported high levels of loneliness had a 68% increased risk of hospitalization, a 57% higher risk of emergency department visits, and a 26% increased risk of outpatient visits, compared with patients reporting low levels of loneliness.[136] Combining data from 13 studies on heart failure patients, researchers found that poor social connection is associated with a 55% greater risk of hospital readmission.[137] This was consistent across both objective and perceived social isolation, including living alone, lack of social support, and poor social network. Furthermore, evidence suggests that people who are less socially connected, particularly those living alone, may be less likely to make it to the hospital, increasing their risk of dying from a cardiac event.[138] Conversely, a heart attack is less likely to be fatal for people living with others or who have more social contacts, perhaps because of the immediate response and availability of help during the event.[138]

Hypertension

High blood pressure (hypertension) is one of the leading causes of cardiovascular disease.[139] Several studies demonstrate that the more social support one has, the greater the reduction in the possibility of developing high blood pressure, even in populations who are at higher risk for the condition, such as Black Americans. Greater social support in this group is associated with a 36% lower risk of high blood pressure in the long-term.[140] Among older adults, the effect of social isolation on hypertension risk is even greater than that of other major clinical risk factors such as diabetes.[59]

KEY DATA

A synthesis of data across 16 independent longitudinal studies shows poor social relationships (social isolation, poor social support, loneliness) were associated with a 29% increase in the risk of heart disease and a 32% increase in the risk of stroke.

Our Epidemic of Loneliness and Isolation: The U.S. Surgeon General's Advisory on the Healing Effects of Social Connection and Community

26

Since high blood pressure most often doesn't have symptoms, it is possible for people to be unaware of even severe underlying cases.[141] The disorder may remain undiagnosed for years, which can elevate the risk for a wide range of physiological complications.[141] However, among older adults, people with higher perceived emotional support from family and friends, and with frequent exposure to health-related information within their social networks, are significantly less likely to have undiagnosed and uncontrolled hypertension.[142]

The results of many research studies also reflect a strong correlation between social connection and high blood pressure control. Regular participation in two or more social or community-based groups[143]; emotional and informational support from family, friends, professional contacts, community organizations, and peer groups[144-146]; and frequent network interactions[142] may improve hypertension management, including following treatment recommendations and long-term lifestyle adjustments. Findings from the National Social Life, Health, and Aging Project (NSHAP) suggest a "causal role of social connections in reducing hypertension," particularly in adults over the age of 50.[59]

Diabetes

Evidence gathered over the last 25 years has demonstrated that social context is important to the development and management of diabetes.[147] Population-based studies show the impact of social connection on the development of type 2 diabetes and diabetic complications.[148,149] For example, social disconnection (poor structural social support[150] and living alone[151] in men, low emotional support in women,[152] and not having a current partner in women older than 70[153]) has been linked to an increased risk for the development of type 2 diabetes. Furthermore, living alone increased the risk of developing type 2 diabetes among women with impaired glucose tolerance.[154]

By contrast, social connection has been associated with better self-rated health and disease management among individuals with diabetes.[155-157] The involvement and support of family members has also been repeatedly shown to improve disease management and the health of people with type 1 diabetes and type 2 diabetes.[147] Whereas, smaller social network size has been associated with newly diagnosed type 2 diabetes and complications from diabetes.[148,149] These associations between social connection and broader diabetic outcomes including diagnosed pre-diabetes and type 2 diabetes, macrovascular complications (e.g., heart attack, stroke) and microvascular complications (e.g., diabetic retinopathy, impaired sensitivity in the feet, and signs of kidney disease) were independent of blood sugar (glucose) control, quality of life, and other cardiac risk factors.[148,149]

What explains this phenomenon? Diabetic outcomes may be better among people who are more socially connected due to better diabetic management behaviors and patient self-care such as medication adherence, physical activity, diet, and foot care. For example, in a meta-analysis of 28 studies, social support from family and friends was significantly associated with better self-care, particularly blood sugar monitoring.[158] Finally, evidence from the National Health and Nutrition Examination Survey found that among older adults with diabetes, those with a large social support network size (at least six close friends) had a reduced risk of all-cause mortality.[159]

Infectious Diseases

People who are less socially connected may have increased susceptibility and weaker immune responses when they are exposed to infectious diseases. In a series of studies examining factors that contribute to illness after exposure to viruses like the common cold and flu, loneliness and poor social support were found to significantly contribute to the development and severity of the illnesses.[42,160] In one study where participants were exposed to a common cold virus, individuals with social ties to six or more diverse social roles (e.g., parent, spouse, friend, family, co-worker, group membership) had a four-fold lower risk of developing a cold when compared to people who had ties to fewer (1-3) diverse social roles.[161] These effects cannot be explained by previous exposure, since those who are more socially connected have stronger immune responses independent of baseline antibody count—suggesting stronger immune responses even when exposed to new viruses.[42] A study conducted on immune responses to the COVID-19 vaccine found that a lack of social connection with neighbors and resultant loneliness was associated with weaker antibody responses to the vaccine.[162]

KEY DATA

50%

Chronic loneliness and social isolation can increase the risk of developing dementia by approximately 50% in older adults.

Cognitive Function

Substantial evidence also links social isolation and loneliness with accelerated cognitive decline and an increased risk of dementia in older adults,[10,41] including Alzheimer's disease.[163] Chronic loneliness and social isolation can increase the risk of developing dementia by approximately 50% in older adults, even after controlling for demographics and health status.[41] A study that followed older adults over 12 years found that cognitive abilities declined 20% faster among those who reported loneliness.[164]

When taken together, this evidence consistently shows that wider social networks and more frequent social engagements with friends and family are associated with better cognitive function and may protect against the risk of dementia.[40,165] This suggests that investments in social connection may be an important public health response to cognitive decline.

Depression and Anxiety

Depression and anxiety are often characterized by social withdrawal, which increases the risk for both social isolation and loneliness; however, social isolation and loneliness also predict increased risk for developing depression and anxiety and can worsen these conditions over time. A systematic review of multiple longitudinal studies found that the odds of developing depression in adults is more than double among people who report feeling lonely often, compared to those who rarely or never feel lonely.[39] Furthermore, in older adults, both social isolation and loneliness have been shown to independently increase the likelihood of depression or anxiety.[166] These findings are also consistent among younger people. A review of 63 studies concluded that loneliness and social isolation among children and adolescents increase the risk of depression and anxiety, and that this risk remained high even up to nine years later.[167]

KEY DATA

Loneliness and social isolation among children and adolescents increase the risk of depression and anxiety.

Importantly, social connection also seems to protect against depression even in people with a higher probability of developing the condition. For example, frequently confiding in others is associated with up to 15% reduced odds of developing depression among people who are already at higher risk due to their history of traumatic or otherwise adverse life experiences.[168]

Suicidality and Self-Harm

> "Social isolation is arguably the strongest and most reliable predictor of suicidal ideation, attempts, and lethal suicidal behavior among samples varying in age, nationality, and clinical severity."[169]
>
> 2010 Study, "The Interpersonal Theory of Suicide"

While many factors may contribute to suicide, more than a century of research has demonstrated significant links between a lack of social connection and death by suicide. This research suggests that social connection may protect against suicide as a cause of death, especially for men.

One study found that among men, deaths due to suicide are associated with loneliness and more strongly with indicators of objective isolation such as living alone.[170] In this study of over 500,000 middle-aged adults, the probability of dying by suicide more than doubled among men who lived alone. The same study showed that for women loneliness was significantly associated with hospitalization for self-harm.[170] Further, when examining suicidality among nursing home and other long-term care facility residents,[171] cancer patients,[172] older adults,[173] and adolescents,[174] systematic reviews of studies on loneliness, social isolation, and low social support were associated with suicidal ideation. These links may result from a low sense of belonging and perceiving oneself as a burden to others.[169]

Loneliness and low social support are also associated with increased risk of self-harm. In a review of 40 studies of more than 60,000 older adults, an increase in loneliness was reported to be among the primary motivations for self-harm.[175]

Given the totality of the evidence, social connection may be one of the strongest protective factors against self-harm and suicide among people with and without serious underlying mental health challenges.

Social Connection Influences Health Through Multiple Pathways

While the effects of social connection on health are clear, research also helps explain how our level of social connection ultimately results in better or worse health. A key part of the explanation involves understanding how social connection influences behavioral, biological, and psychological processes, which in turn influence health outcomes. A large body of evidence has identified several plausible pathways (see **Figure 5**).[59,176-180]

Our Epidemic of Loneliness and Isolation: The U.S. Surgeon General's Advisory on the Healing Effects of Social Connection and Community

30

How Does Social Connection Influence Health?

Social connection influences health through **three principal pathways:** biology, psychology, and behavior.

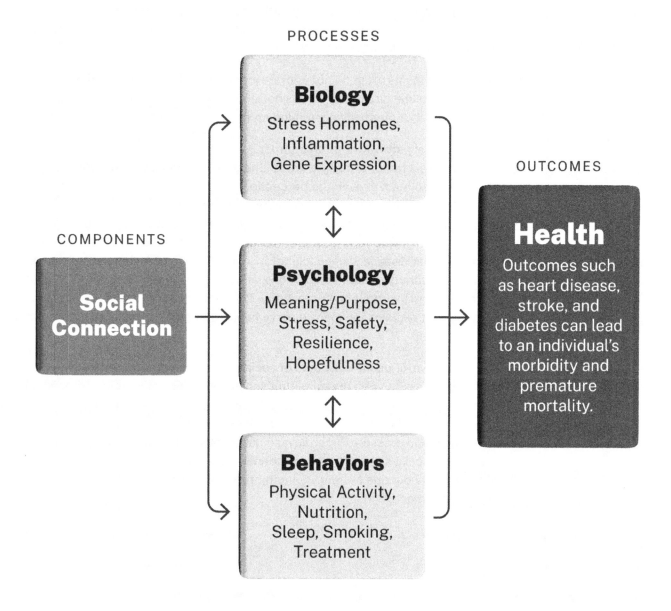

Source: Holt-Lunstad J. The Major Health Implications of Social Connection. *Current Directions in Psychological Science.* 2021;30(3):251-259.

Office *of the* **U.S. Surgeon General**

FIGURE 4: How Does Social Connection Influence Health?

Social Connection Influences Biological Processes

The role of social connection on biology emerges early in life and continues across the life course, contributing to risk and protection from disease.[59] Several reviews document that social connection can influence health through specific biological pathways, including cardiovascular and neuroendocrine dysregulation,[181] immunity,[42,177,182-184] and gut-microbiome interactions.[185,186] Because regulation of these systems is critical for good health, the documented influence between social connection and these biological pathways likely explains the impact on the risk of the development of disease.

Biological systems often do not operate independently. This means that increases in blood pressure, circulating stress hormones, and inflammation may occur simultaneously, potentially compounding risk across several biological systems.[187]

One biological pathway of great interest is inflammation, given that it has been implicated as a factor in many chronic illnesses.[188] Evidence shows that being objectively isolated, or even the perception of isolation, can increase inflammation to the same degree as physical inactivity.[59] Similarly, lower social support is associated with higher inflammation.[189,190] Chronic inflammation throughout the body has been linked to various chronic illnesses across the lifespan, such as cardiovascular disease, cancer, diabetes, depression, and Alzheimer's disease, as well as a variety of mental, cognitive, and physical health outcomes[188,191] that increase the risk of premature mortality. Thus, inflammation may be a common pathway that explains the many diverse health outcomes associated with isolation and loneliness.

The protective, or positive, effects of social connection may operate on biological systems in a similar way, meaning that social connection may reduce the risk of disease by reducing biological system dysregulation. For example, increased levels of social connection can improve various biomarkers of cardiovascular functioning, including blood pressure,[192] cardiovascular reactivity,[193] and oxidative stress.[194] In addition, social support and social bonding are associated with better regulation of the neuroendocrine system, including the role of oxytocin in both early life and adult attachment.[181,195-197]

Social Connection Influences Psychological Processes

Social connection can also influence health through psychological processes, such as the sense of meaning and purpose. Adults across the globe rate their social relationships, particularly with family and close friends, as the most important source of meaning, purpose, and motivation in their lives.[198] A sense of meaning positively contributes to health because it motivates greater self-regulation in pursuing goals—including health goals.[180] Furthermore, evidence suggests that individuals with higher purpose and perceived emotional and practical support from their social networks are more likely to engage in health-promoting behaviors, such as the use of preventive health care services.[199,200]

Other psychological processes, including the perception of stress, may also have implications for health because they can influence our biology and behavior. For example, higher social connection provides increased opportunities for and access to support, thus reducing the likelihood of perceiving challenging situations as stressful and helping us cope with stressful situations to minimize their impact.[28,201] Conversely, being isolated or in poor quality relationships can increase the likelihood that one perceives potential challenges as stressful. This stress may be heightened because the individual has less support and fewer resources to draw upon to cope with the situation.[28,201]

Though certain forms of manageable, short-term challenges can boost performance and motivation in day-to-day life, chronic stress and cumulative biologic burden can contribute to worsened health outcomes. For example, stress can contribute to poorer health-related behaviors, cause disruptions in brain development, and increase the risk for mental health conditions and other health problems such as obesity, heart disease, and diabetes.[202-205] Additionally, while loneliness, poor-quality relationships, and social negativity can aggravate stress responses and influence long-term health outcomes,[206] being more socially connected can buffer against maladaptive stress responses and the negative health effects of stress.[28,201]

A sense of meaning positively contributes to health because it motivates greater self-regulation in pursuing goals — including health goals.

Our Epidemic of Loneliness and Isolation: The U.S. Surgeon General's Advisory on the Healing Effects of Social Connection and Community

33

Social Connection Influences Behaviors

Social connection is also significantly associated with a number of health-related behaviors, including lifestyle behaviors (e.g., diet, exercise, sleep),[207-210] and treatment adherence (e.g., taking medication as directed, engaging in recommended prevention measures)[144,199,211,212] which ultimately influence our health and longevity. Social influence can be direct—loved ones encouraging one to get more sleep or reminding one to take their medication—or subtle, through social norms that communicate approval or disapproval of certain behaviors (like vaccination, smoking, exercise). In fact, evidence shows people are far more likely to be physically active if their peers and friends also exercise,[213,214] and they are more likely to stop smoking themselves if their social contacts do so as well.[215] However, they are also less likely to stop smoking if they are in close connection to others who smoke, or even at risk for relapse if they had successfully quit smoking previously.[216,217] Thus, it is clear that it is not just the presence of social connection and social support but the nature of the behaviors and norms in one's social network that influence health-related behaviors.

Individual Educational and Economic Benefits

The benefits of social connection extend beyond the well-being of individuals' health to quality of life, education, employment, and economic outcomes. Just as with health, those who lack sufficient social connection, whether because they are isolated, lonely, or in poor-quality relationships, seem to be at higher risk for poorer outcomes in these aspects of life as well.

Educational Benefits

Research shows that children and adolescents who enjoy positive relationships with their peers, parents, and teachers experience improved academic outcomes. For example, a review of youth mentoring programs found a positive association between mentoring programs intended to promote positive youth outcomes and improved school attendance, grades, and academic achievement test scores.[218] Further, school and family connectedness during adolescent years may predict subsequent positive outcomes in early adulthood, including a higher likelihood of graduating college and attaining a 4-year college degree.[219]

In contrast, the lack of quality social connections inhibits student progression even in higher education settings. For example, among medical students, feeling socially isolated is associated with dropping out.[45] The lack of social connection is cited as a prime reason for leaving a program.

Economic Benefits

Supportive and inclusive relationships at work are associated with employee job satisfaction, creativity, competence, and better job performance.[220-224] Quality social support, social integration, and regular communication among co-workers of all levels are key in preventing chronic work stress and workplace burnout.[48,225] These resources may even be linked to shorter recovery times and less missed work after work-related injuries or illnesses.[225,226] Workplace connectedness is also associated with enhanced individual innovation, engagement, and quality of work, all of which can influence career advancements, income, and overall economic stability.[220,223]

Social connection outside the workplace also plays an important role in an individual's economic situation. Diverse social networks that facilitate interaction and relationship-building among people of differing socioeconomic status (SES) may provide opportunities for individuals from lower SES backgrounds to gain stronger footing in the labor market and obtain higher-paying jobs.[227,228] Such bridging, cross-class ties are among the most important predictors of upward economic mobility.

Additionally, activities that better connect individuals to one another, including immersion in local community-based activities or volunteering, can also equip individuals with desirable skills that make them more employable, and significantly increase the likelihood of unemployed individuals becoming employed.[229-231]

Our Epidemic of Loneliness and Isolation: The U.S. Surgeon General's Advisory on the Healing Effects of Social Connection and Community

35

Chapter 3   How Social Connection Impacts Communities

Decades of research across disciplines such as political science, economics, sociology, behavioral science, and public health, among others, have examined the relationship between group social connection and population health and well-being.[13,15,17,34-36,49,50] Though variation exists across studies and methodologies, the cumulative evidence generally points to the same conclusion: higher levels of social connectedness suggest better community outcomes, ranging from population health to community safety, resilience, prosperity, and representative government; while lower levels of social connectedness suggest worse outcomes in each of these areas. These studies establish that social connection is vital not only to our individual physical, mental, and emotional health, but also to the health and well-being of our communities.

This chapter explores what it means to be a socially connected community and examines the evidence that more connected communities benefit from higher levels of well-being. The chapter also addresses the potential harms of negative social connection for community and societal well-being.

Socially Connected Communities

The scientific literature on social connection has defined "community" in many ways.[232,233] Broadly, the term refers to a group of people with a characteristic in common. For the purpose of this advisory, however, the terms "community" and "communities" refer to a shared geographic location—neighborhoods, towns, cities. This chapter summarizes research that pertains to in-person social connection and the benefits that exist within place-based communities.

This does not diminish other types of communities (including those online) that can also provide support and other important elements of social connection. However, in-depth review of these types of communities is beyond the scope of this advisory and requires additional research.

Social capital is a key concept that researchers have identified as an important characteristic for understanding the social connectedness of communities. The definition and measurement of social capital varies by discipline, but broadly, social capital may be understood as "the resources to which individuals and groups have access through their social networks."[13,14] The term social capital is often used as an umbrella for both social support and social cohesion.[15]

Social support refers to the perceived or actual availability of emotional, informational, or tangible resources from other individuals in one's social network.[10,28] **Social cohesion** refers to the sense of solidarity within groups, marked by strong social connections and high levels of social participation, that generates trust, norms of reciprocity, and a sense of belonging.[13,15,17,18]

Trust is a critical component of socially connected communities and a subjective indicator frequently used to measure social capital.[15] Again, the scientific literature defines trust in many ways, but, broadly, it refers to an individual's expectation of positive intent and benevolence from the actions of others.[29-31] Trust is an attitude that informs behavior towards unknown people (**generalized trust**), towards a known individual or group (**particularized trust**), or towards organizations and government (**institutional trust**).[29,234] It underlies communication and cooperation, both elements of social cohesion and social support. Higher levels of trust have been linked to improved population health, economic prosperity, and social functioning.[15,235]

The **social infrastructure** of a community shapes its social capital. This refers to the programs (such as volunteer organizations, sports groups, religious groups, and member associations), policies (like public transportation, housing, and education), and physical elements of a community (such as libraries, parks, green spaces, and playgrounds) that facilitate bringing people together. Social infrastructure may help a community by providing opportunities to foster social connections among residents, local leaders, and community-serving organizations. As social networks grow in size, diversity, and strength, this produces greater levels of social support and social cohesion and builds social capital for a community.

Because belonging to a group is generally adaptive and improves survival, people have a natural tendency to build and maintain relationships with those who are most like themselves (e.g., those with similar educational backgrounds, incomes, professions, or family status).[236] This type of social connection, defined as **bonding social capital**, is important and can provide the support and resources needed not only to prevent or reduce loneliness and social isolation but also to contribute to fulfillment and well-being.[237,238]

Research suggests that diversifying social relationships to include connections with people who are outside of your group (**bridging social capital**), as well as connections between people of differing power status in the community (**linking social capital**) are also associated with improved community health and well-being.[13,237-239] Examples of these types of relationships include cultivating intergenerational friendships (bridging) or developing programs like a mentorship exchange between youth and local employers (linking).

Larger and more diverse social networks, with a mixture of types of relationships, can provide access to more varied types of social support and generate greater levels of social capital. Furthermore, interacting with people from diverse backgrounds can help to stimulate creative thinking and encourage the consideration of different perspectives, leading to better problem-solving and decision-making.[240] Finally, social interactions with neighbors and other community members—like small gestures such as smiling at a passerby or brief conversations at the bank, post office, grocery store, or local coffee shop—can foster a sense of interpersonal trust and create and maintain norms of reciprocity.[12,241] This can also increase **empathy**, one of the best documented sources of altruism, by enhancing understanding with one another, supporting the development of shared identities and affiliations, and facilitating cooperation and beneficial interactions across individuals and groups.[7,8] This helps to generate more social capital for the broader community.

These community interactions can be associated with a positive reinforcing cycle. As this chapter illustrates, individuals who immerse themselves in community-based activities are more likely to experience stronger feelings of social belonging and develop trusting relationships with fellow community members. This can lead people to more readily contribute their time and resources back to their communities. When community-based participation becomes the norm, social networks grow and produce high levels of trust among themselves, which facilitates the efficient exchange of information and sharing of resources within a community.

The Benefits of More Connected Communities

Population Health

Communities with higher levels of social connection typically enjoy significantly better health outcomes than communities that have lower levels.[16,17,242-244] Studies find that community-level social capital is positively associated with a reduced burden of disease and risk for all-cause mortality.[17,243,245-247] A meta-analysis of several studies looking at the cumulative effects across multiple indicators of social capital on all-cause mortality and general health found that on average, a one-unit increase in social capital increases the likelihood of survival by 17% and of self-reporting good health by 29%.[243] In a separate study using data from 39 states, the authors found a dose-response relationship between the extent of social capital within a community and age-adjusted mortality.[248] A 10% increase (one standard deviation) in the proportion of residents in each state who felt that other people could be trusted was associated with an 8% decline in overall mortality.[248] Another study found that those with very strong perceptions of community belonging—an indicator of social cohesion—reported very good or excellent health at a rate 2.6 times higher than those with very low perceptions of belongingness.[245] This was true even after adjusting for demographic variables, health and health behaviors, and the built environment. Finally, communities with higher levels of social capital are also more likely to see decreased hospital readmission rates.[249]

KEY DATA

On average, a one-unit increase in social capital increases the likelihood of survival by 17% and of self-reporting good health by 29%.

The positive effects of social capital on health are not only evident when added up across individuals. Synergistic effects among various aspects of social capital also exist and impact community-wide health outcomes. Connected individuals who leverage available social capital resources to improve their health-related behaviors or collectively reform their community culture can generate downstream improvements in overall population-level health.

For example, personal biases and fears about highly stigmatized diseases such as HIV create barriers to health care and social inclusion for individuals living with HIV.[250,251] A review of multiple studies shows that high levels of social capital in high-risk populations can buffer against those harmful social barriers and significantly increase the likelihood of HIV prevention behaviors.[250,252,253] In turn, members of highly connected communities are more likely to participate in health-protective efforts and seek care when needed, thereby decreasing the disease burden and risk of disease transmission among the whole population. Similarly, more connected communities have higher utilization of immunization services, and are more likely to adopt recommended health-protective behaviors— all of which benefit the broader community.[254-258]

Evidence also shows that stronger social bonds and social capital in communities increase the likelihood that local community groups and health care institutions will build population health-focused partnerships.[259] These partnerships rely on the existing mutual trust and reciprocity within community settings to increase engagement opportunities within the population and improve access to health care in low-resource populations.[259,260]

On the other hand, several reports have found that lower community social connection is linked to poorer health outcomes. This was made clear when examining the spread of the COVID-19 virus.[261-264] One study in the United States compared changes in the county-level spread of COVID-19 against several measures of social capital.[265] These included family structure and involvement, trust in community institutions, popularity of volunteerism, levels of participation in political discussions and voting efforts, and cohesion among community members. After controlling for potential alternative explanatory factors, the researchers found that lower levels of social capital were associated with a higher number of cases and deaths from COVID-19 infection.[265] Further, counties with strong social ties experienced fewer deaths during the COVID-19 pandemic.[263,265] Relatedly, an international study of COVID-19 infection and fatality rates across 177 countries also observed a statistically significant association between greater interpersonal and government trust and lower infection rates.[266]

Natural Hazard Preparation and Resilience

A community's resilience to natural hazard events such as earthquakes, tsunamis, hurricanes, large-scale flooding, and fires depends upon the collective ability of individuals, households, and institutions to prepare for anticipated events, adapt to and withstand changing conditions, and recover rapidly following disruption.[267,268]

Studies show that neighbors are often the first to respond in disaster situations, even before trained emergency professionals, because they are physically nearby.[34] Growing evidence suggests that in neighborhoods and communities where people know one another and are connected to community institutions (like service organizations, religious groups, or community-based organizations) people prepare for, respond to, and recover more quickly from natural hazards than those with lower levels of social connection.[232,269]

In such connected communities, it is more likely that people will share their knowledge and informal resources with neighbors, prepare for natural hazards, comply with emergency procedures including evacuation, and engage in coordination of emergency response efforts after natural hazard events.[35,270]

Our Epidemic of Loneliness and Isolation: The U.S. Surgeon General's Advisory on the Healing Effects of Social Connection and Community

40

Further, high levels of social connection reduce the exodus of people immediately following a natural hazard, preserve valuable social capital like social support and interpersonal trust, enable neighbors to provide aid to one another, and allow communities to overcome collective action problems such as coordinating recovery and rebuilding.[35] Despite these benefits of connection within and for neighborhood communities, only 3 in 10 Americans report knowing all or most of their neighbors.[72]

Community Safety

Not only do higher levels of social connection within a community correspond to better health and disaster outcomes, but they are also associated with lower levels of community violence.[271-274] One recent study on community violence showed that a one standard deviation increase in social connectedness was associated with a 21% reduction in murders and a 20% reduction in motor vehicle thefts.[271] The Project on Human Development in Chicago Neighborhoods longitudinal study that began in the late 1990s found that neighborhoods with higher perceptions of social cohesion and where residents felt a "willingness to act" on behalf of community members (**collective efficacy**) were more likely to have reduced levels of crime and residents were more likely to feel safer.[6] Many subsequent analyses have confirmed the association between social connection, greater perceived collective efficacy, and community safety. Recent studies have found that greater perceived collective efficacy,[49,275,276] trust,[277] and social norms on violence as unacceptable behavior can be protective factors against community violence.[278,279] Fostering social connection is not a singular solution to community violence; however, it does play an instrumental role in prevention and response.

Economic Prosperity

Economic prosperity, including economic development, employment, the sharing of economic opportunities or information, and overall economic connectedness, is a key measure of the value that exists within a given society. Evidence illustrates that connected communities generally experience higher levels of economic prosperity. For example, an analysis of economic factors across the U.S. found that communities with higher social capital levels experienced greater resilience against unemployment between 2006 and 2010 and were able to weather the recession more successfully.[280] In addition, a three-year study of 26 cities in the U.S. found that those with the highest levels of resident attachment experienced the greatest growth in GDP during the study period.[281]

Further, members of these connected communities are more likely to recommend job and educational opportunities to one another, collaborate on ideas for innovation, build partnerships for local businesses, and directly advance economic progress in their communities.[280,282] In addition, longitudinal evidence shows that civic engagement, another form of community participation, in adolescence and early adulthood positively predicts educational attainment and income potential in adulthood.[283] In this way, local community participation may also influence socioeconomic mobility of individuals across their lifespan and also reduce large-scale socioeconomic disparities.

> Local community participation may influence socioeconomic mobility of individuals across their lifespan and also reduce large-scale socioeconomic disparities.

In contrast to the clear benefits of community connectedness, the consequences of disconnection on community prosperity can be detrimental. Long-standing systemic disinvestment, inequitable zoning laws, underdeveloped transportation systems, and residential segregation can perpetuate chronic poverty and isolate entire neighborhoods or towns from more prosperous local economies.[36] On the other hand, cross-class exposure could have positive impacts on economic mobility across generations.[227] For example, if children of low socioeconomic backgrounds had the share of high socioeconomic friends comparable to that of the average child with a high socioeconomic background, these children would increase their incomes in adulthood by an average of 20%.[227] Pro-connection policies and practices can promote economic prosperity in communities harmed by structural barriers and eliminate such obstacles toward prosperity.

Civic Engagement and Representative Government

Higher levels of social connection are associated with increased levels of civic engagement (defined as "actions to address issues of public concern") and more representative government.[15,50,284] Emerging evidence has shown that civic engagement helps to develop "empathy, problem solving, [and] cooperation" among community members.[285] One study showed that higher levels of family and community connection during adolescence predicted civic engagement outcomes in young adulthood including a greater likelihood of voting and involvement in social action and conversation groups.[286] Further examples of civic engagement include registering to vote and voting, participating in advocacy groups or clubs,

Our Epidemic of Loneliness and Isolation: The U.S. Surgeon General's Advisory on the Healing Effects of Social Connection and Community

42

and connecting to information and current events. In addition, studies show that group membership and social networks strongly influence the decision to participate in the political process.[287] Moreover, in a positive cycle, research suggests that greater civic engagement can lead to policies and programs that better reflect the will of a community's residents, which in turn can promote continued and increased civic engagement.[15,284,288,289]

The Potential Negative Side of Social Connection

Our fundamental human need for belonging is so strong that we may seek it out even in ways that may be unhealthy to ourselves or to our broader community. This can include participation in gangs and joining extremist or other harmful groups. Our natural tendency to associate with those most like us can be manipulated, with potentially negative consequences for individual and community well-being. When there are scarce resources, this can also lead to competition among various groups, leading to an "us" versus "them" mentality.

We tend to view our own group as more favorable and deserving than members of other groups.[290] This can result in distrust and rejection of outsiders.[291] In addition, among highly cohesive groups, there are also strong pressures to conform to the group norms[292]—often with high costs like rejection or ostracization if one doesn't comply. While high cohesion and conformity to group norms can be healthy and productive in many cases, among some groups, these social pressures may justify, rationalize, or encourage unhealthy, unsafe, or unfair behaviors such as binge drinking, violence, and discrimination.[274,292]

Our Epidemic of Loneliness and Isolation: The U.S. Surgeon General's Advisory on the Healing Effects of Social Connection and Community

43

Societal Polarization

One consequence of the natural tendency for people to build and maintain relationships with those who are like themselves is the risk for exacerbating polarization in our discourse and in society—potentially leading to poorer outcomes for broader society.[237,293,294]

"Core discussion networks," are circles of people who have conversations on timely but difficult topics such as politics, finances, world events, religion, health, and more. The nature, size, and diversity of these discussion networks are important to how individuals form opinions, attitudes, and awareness of differing perspectives.[295] They ultimately foster political tolerance.[296] Generally, the size and diversity of core discussion networks have been shrinking substantially over the recent decades.[297] One survey of 1,055 U.S. adults during the 2016 U.S. presidential election found that core discussion networks were smaller than in any other observed period and that the proportion of individuals with the same political preference within core discussion networks was higher than reported previously.[298]

KEY DATA

2x

Growing ideological divisions in America are fueling skepticism and even animosity between groups across the political divide: sentiments of enmity and disapproval between Democrats and Republicans more than doubled between 1994 and 2014.

As discussion networks shrink and become more politically homogenous while society becomes more polarized, it is perhaps not surprising that almost 6 in 10 U.S. adults report that it is "stressful and frustrating" to talk about politics with people who hold different political opinions.[299] A recent survey found that 64% of individuals believe that people are incapable of having constructive and civil debates about issues on which they disagree.[300] Additionally, growing ideological divisions in the U.S. are fueling skepticism and even animosity between groups across the political divide—sentiments of enmity and disapproval between Democrats and Republicans more than doubled between 1994 and 2014.[67] Polarization can lead to identity-based extremism and violence, pointing to the urgent need to foster social connection across group-based ideological differences through **bridging social capital**.[293,294,301]

Chapter 4

A National Strategy to Advance Social Connection

The world is just beginning to recognize the vital importance of social connection. While the evidence of the severe consequences of social isolation, loneliness, and overall social disconnection has been building for decades, a global pandemic crystallized and accelerated the urgency for the United States to establish a National Strategy to Advance Social Connection. Such a strategy not only recognizes the critical importance of advancing social connection, but also serves as a commitment to invest in and take actions establishing that our connection with others is a core value of this nation.

As this advisory has shown, fulfilling connections are a critical and often underappreciated contributor to individual and population health and longevity, safety, prosperity, and well-being. On the other hand, social disconnection contributes to many poor health outcomes, and even to premature death. Sadly, around 50% of adults in the U.S. reported being lonely in recent years[1-3] — and that was even before COVID-19 separated so many of us from our friends, loved ones, and support systems. Our bonds with others and our community are also part of this equation. Research has shown that more connected communities enjoy higher levels of well-being. The converse is also true. How do we put this important information to practical use in our society? What actionable steps can we take to enhance social connection so that we can all enjoy its benefits?

A National Strategy to Advance Social Connection is the critical next step to catalyze action essential to our nation's health, safety, and prosperity. The strategy includes six foundational pillars and a series of key recommendations, organized according to stakeholder group, to support a whole-of-society approach to advancing social connection. Individuals and organizations can use this framework to propel the critical work of reversing these worrisome trends and strengthening social connection and community.

Doing so won't always be easy. Fostering greater connection requires widespread individual and institutional action. It demands our sustained investment, effort, and focus. But it will be worth it, because when we each take these critical steps, we are choosing better lives, and to create a better world for all.

Such a world, where we recognize that relationships are just as essential to our well-being as the air we breathe and the food we eat, is a world where everyone is healthier, physically and mentally. It is a world where we respect and value one another, where we look out for one another, and where we create opportunities to uplift one another. A world where our highs are higher because we celebrate them together; where our lows are more manageable because we respond to them together; and where our recovery is faster because we grieve and rebuild together.

It is a world where we are strong enough to hold our differences, where we are more comfortable and motivated to engage civically, and where our leaders and institutions are more representative of the people they serve. It is a world where we trust one another, where we feel safe to challenge one another and change our minds, and where prosperity and progress are not the privilege of the few but accessible to all.

We can choose, in short, to take the core values that make us strong—love, kindness, respect, service, and commitment to one another—and reflect them in the world we build for ourselves and our children. This strategy shows us how to create the connected lives and the connected world we need.

Benefits of a National Strategy to Advance Social Connection

- **Cultivating individual health and well-being** across physical and mental health and educational and economic outcomes. This enables individuals to be happier, more prosperous, and to contribute more fully to society.

- **Strengthening community health, safety, and prosperity** by cultivating social cohesion and social capital within and across communities. This enables communities to overcome adversity and thrive.

- **Building resilience for the next set of challenges** such as natural hazards, pandemics, and safety threats. This enables society to withstand unanticipated crises through stronger recovery and resilience.

- **Advancing civic engagement and representative government** by fostering a more engaged citizenry. This enables policies and programs to better reflect the will of a community and its individuals.

Office *of the*
U.S. Surgeon General

The Six Pillars to Advance
Social Connection

1

Strengthen Social Infrastructure in Local Communities

Design the built environment to promote social connection

Establish and scale community connection programs

Invest in local institutions that bring people together

2

Enact Pro-Connection Public Policies

Adopt a "Connection-in-All-Policies" approach

Advance policies that minimize harm from disconnection

Establish cross-departmental leadership at all levels of government

3

Mobilize the Health Sector

Train health care providers

Assess and support patients

Expand public health surveillance and interventions

4

Reform Digital Environments

Require data transparency

Establish and implement safety standards

Support development of pro-connection technologies

5

Deepen Our Knowledge

Develop and coordinate a national research agenda

Accelerate research funding

Increase public awareness

6

Build a Culture of Connection

Cultivate values of kindness, respect, service, and commitment to one another

Model connection values in positions of leadership and influence

Expand conversation on social connection in schools, workplaces, and communities

FIGURE 6: The Six Pillars to Advance Social Connection

**The Six Pillars
to Advance
Social Connection**

Strengthen Social Infrastructure in Local Communities

- Design the built environment to promote social connection

- Establish and scale community connection programs

- Invest in local institutions that bring people together

Many factors that influence social connection are environmental. Decisions about the layout of our cities, from the usability and reach of public transportation to the design of housing and green spaces, have a direct effect on social interaction in a community.[302,303] This is why strengthening social infrastructure that promotes social connection is critical to advancing key aspects of community health, resilience, safety, and prosperity. Social infrastructure refers to the programs (such as volunteer organizations, sports groups, religious groups, and member associations), policies (like public transportation, housing, and education), and physical elements of a community (such as libraries, parks, green spaces, and playgrounds) that support the development of social connection.

Investing in local communities and in social infrastructure will fall short if access to the benefits is limited to only some groups. Equitable access to social infrastructure for all groups, including those most at-risk for social disconnection, is foundational to building a connected national and global community, and is essential to this pillar's success.

Moreover, community programs, such as those that connect us to our neighbors, those that help students establish social skills in schools, and those that generate opportunities for high-risk populations to create community, also have a powerful role in building relationships. For example, volunteering is a demonstrated and powerful way to advance connection to one's community and create diverse ties among community members. Finally, institutions that gather individuals for work, study, or prayer, such as workplaces, schools, and faith organizations, can function as sources of positive connection and thereby bolster the community's trust in those institutions and in fellow members. Investing in community connection will be important to repairing divisions and rebuilding trust in each other and our institutions, and is vital to achieving common societal goals.

**The Six Pillars
to Advance
Social Connection**

Pillar 2

Enact Pro-Connection Public Policies

- **Adopt a "Connection-in-All-Policies" approach**

- **Advance policies that minimize harm from disconnection**

- **Establish cross-departmental leadership at all levels of government**

National, state, local, and tribal governments play a critical role in strengthening social connection and community across all sectors. These institutions recognize the importance of social connection to the health of their communities. Policymakers understand that while the effects of social connection may be most evident for health, the drivers of connection and disconnection can be found in all types of policies, from transportation and zoning to nutrition and labor. A "Connection-in-All-Policies" approach recognizes that every sector of society is relevant to social connection, and that policy within each sector may potentially hinder or facilitate connection. Conversely, government has a responsibility to use its authority to monitor and mitigate the public health harm caused by policies, products, and services that drive social disconnection.

Prioritizing social connection in policy agendas and leveraging a "Connection-in-All-Policies" approach requires establishing cross-departmental leadership to develop and oversee an overarching social connection strategy. Diversity, equity, inclusion, and accessibility are critical components of any such strategy. It must recognize that everyone is impacted by social connection, but that some groups may be more disproportionally impacted by some policies. Thus, policymakers must give focused attention to reducing disparities in risk and ensuring equal access to benefits.

**The Six Pillars
to Advance
Social Connection**

Pillar 3

Mobilize the Health Sector

- **Train health care providers**

- **Assess and support patients**

- **Expand public health surveillance and interventions**

Social connection is an independent protective factor, and social isolation and loneliness are independent risk factors for several major health conditions, including cardiovascular disease, dementia, depression, and premature mortality from all causes.[128] While all organizations have a role in addressing social connection, mobilizing the health sector—most notably health care delivery systems and the public health community—is a core pillar of the National Strategy.

It is critical that we invest in health care provider education on the physical and mental health benefits of social connection, as well as the risks associated with social disconnection. We must also create systems that enable and incentivize health care providers to educate patients as part of preventative care, assess for social disconnection, and respond to patients' health-relevant social needs. This can be accomplished both within the medical system and by linking individuals to community-based organizations that can provide necessary support and resources specifically designed to increase social connection.[10,285,304,305] Public health organizations can help track the community prevalence of social disconnection, promote individual best practices, and advance community solutions. By integrating social connection into primary-, secondary-, and tertiary-level prevention and care efforts, we can strive to prevent forms of social disconnection in healthy individuals, mitigate forms of social disconnection early on before they become severe, and provide adequate support for those who are experiencing severe forms of social disconnection.

Our Epidemic of Loneliness and Isolation: The U.S. Surgeon General's Advisory on the Healing Effects of Social Connection and Community

50

**The Six Pillars
to Advance
Social Connection**

Pillar 4

Reform Digital Environments

- **Require data transparency**

- **Establish and implement safety standards**

- **Support development of pro-connection technologies**

The exponential growth of technology crosses geographic borders, broadening communities and opening the world to those with limited access. It has had a tangible impact on how we live and work, from social connectivity, gaming, content sharing, and virality, to flexible work environments and communication.

But these benefits come at a cost. Technology can also distract us and occupy our mental bandwidth, make us feel worse about ourselves or our relationships, and diminish our ability to connect deeply with others. Some technology fans the flames of marginalization and discrimination, bullying, and other forms of severe social negativity.

We must decide how technology is designed and how we use it. There are many ways to minimize harms. We must learn more by requiring data transparency from technology companies. This will enable us to understand their current and long-term effects on social connection, and implement and enforce safety standards (such as age-related protections for young people) that ensure products do not worsen social disconnection. In a positive vein, we should support the development of pro-connection technology to promote healthy social connection, create safe environments for discourse, and safeguard the well-being of users. This should be coupled with the public's greater ability to avoid or limit their own uses.

Finally, we need to recognize the unique aspects of digital technology that may differ from other modes of connecting socially. The modality of delivery matters, and should be strategically and explicitly acknowledged and evaluated.

**The Six Pillars
to Advance
Social Connection**

Pillar 5

Deepen our Knowledge

- **Develop and coordinate a national research agenda**

- **Accelerate research funding**

- **Increase public awareness**

This Surgeon General's Advisory outlines a summary of the evidence about how social connection and disconnection impact individual and community health and overall well-being. The totality of this evidence illustrates that urgent action is needed, including additional research to further advance our understanding of the causes and consequences of social connection, trends, populations at risk, and the effectiveness of interventions and other efforts to advance connection.

As a next step, relevant stakeholders, including government, policymakers, practitioners, and researchers, should work together to establish a research agenda focused on addressing identified gaps in the evidence base, fund research at levels commensurate with the seriousness of the problem, and create a plan to increase research coordination. Deepening our knowledge of social connection and disconnection also requires us to further refine and expand our capacity to measure these states via agreed upon standardized metrics. As individuals, communities, institutions, and governments implement the pillars of the National Strategy, consistent measurement will be critical to better understanding the driving forces of connection and disconnection, and how we can be more effective and efficient in addressing these states.

Public understanding of the essential role of social connection in health and well-being is critical to this pillar. Social connection should be included as a key driver of health in formal health education, from elementary to professional school curricula. It is also imperative that we share this knowledge beyond health professionals. Public awareness and education of the drivers and solutions of connection and disconnection will be a critical foundation to support sustained policy and cultural change.

**The Six Pillars
to Advance
Social Connection**

Pillar 6

Cultivate a Culture of Connection

- **Cultivate values of kindness, respect, service, and commitment to one another**

- **Model connection values in positions of leadership and influence**

- **Expand conversations on social connection in schools, workplaces, and communities**

A culture of connection is vital to creating the changes needed in society. While formal programs and policies can be impactful, the informal practices of everyday life—the norms and culture of how we engage one another—significantly influence social connection. These shared beliefs and values drive our individual and collective behaviors that then shape programs and policies. We cannot be successful in the other pillars without this underlying culture of connection.

Such a culture of connection rests on core values of kindness, respect, service, and commitment to one another. Everyone contributes to the collective culture of social connection by regularly practicing these values. Advancing this culture requires individuals and leaders to seek opportunities to do so in public and private dialogue, schools, workplaces, and in the forces that shape our society like media and entertainment, among others. Behaviors are both learned from and reinforced by the groups we participate in and the communities we are a part of. Thus, the more we observe others practicing these values, the more they will be reinforced in us.

All types of leaders and influencers (national, local, political, cultural, corporate, etc.) can use their voices to underscore these core values and model healthy social connection and dialogue. Media and entertainment shape our beliefs through the depiction of stories. These narratives can help individuals see themselves in stories and help to reduce stigma, thus enabling more connection. Further, our institutions should invest time, attention, and resources in ways that demonstrate these values.

Recommendations for Stakeholders to Advance Social Connection

All of us as individuals, organizations, and communities can play a role in increasing and strengthening connection across the nation. This section details recommendations for how each stakeholder group can take action to advance social connection.

What National, Territory, State, Local, and Tribal Governments Can Do

- **Designate social connection a priority** by including it in public health and policy agendas, providing critical resources, and creating strategies to strengthen social connection and community that include clear benchmarks, measurable outcomes, and periodic evaluation.

- **Establish a dedicated leadership position** to work across departments, convene stakeholders, and advance pro-connection policies.

- **Utilize a "Connection-in-All-Policies" Approach** that examines policies across sectors, including health, education, labor, housing, transportation, and the environment, and looks to identify and remedy policies that drive disconnection while advancing those that drive connection. Periodically, evaluate and revise existing policies and programs, and when appropriate, propose new policies to advance social connection. Examples of pro-connection policies include paid leave, which enables individuals to spend time with family during critical early life stages, and increased access to public transit, which allows individuals to physically connect more easily.

- **Monitor and regulate technology** by establishing transparency, accountability, safety, and consumer protections to ensure social health and safety (including for minors) and the ability for independent researchers to evaluate the impact of technology on our health and well-being.[306]

- **Create a standardized national measure or set of measures for social connection and standardized definitions for relevant terms**, in collaboration with the research community. Implement consistent, regular measurement of social connection metrics in current national health surveys, with the ability to capture the level of granularity needed to guide strategic decision-making, planning, and evaluation of strategies.

- **Prioritize research funding** such that research is supported at levels commensurate with the societal impact of loneliness, social isolation, and other forms of social disconnection, and enhance collaboration with researchers to improve research coordination.

- **Launch sustained and inclusive public education and awareness efforts**, including the development of national guidelines for social connection.[307]

- **Invest in social infrastructure at the local level**, including the programs, policies, and physical elements of a community that facilitate bringing people together.

- **Incentivize the assessment and integration of social connection** into health care delivery and public health, including through public insurance coverage and other government funding mechanisms.

- **Increase evaluation and oversight** of policy and programmatic outcomes from public institutions, programs, and services, and make the results available through public facing reports, databases, and other mechanisms. This will help improve existing policies and programs, demonstrate transparency, and increase public trust in institutions.

What Health Workers, Health Care Systems, and Insurers Can Do

- Explicitly **acknowledge social connection as a priority** for health.

- **Provide health professionals with formal training** and continuing education on the health and medical relevance of social connection and risks associated with social disconnection (e.g., isolation, loneliness, low social support, social negativity), as well as advanced training on prevention and interventions.

- Insurance companies should **provide adequate reimbursement** for time spent assessing and addressing concerns about social disconnection (e.g., isolation, loneliness, low social support, poor relationship quality), and incorporate these measurements into value-based payment models.

- **Facilitate inclusion of assessment results in electronic health records.**

- Providers and insurers can **educate and incentivize patients to understand the risks** of, and take action to address, inadequate social connection, with a particular focus on at-risk individuals, including but not limited to those with physical or mental health conditions or disabilities, financial insecurity, those who live alone, single parents, and both younger and aging populations.

- **Integrate social connection into patient care** in primary-, secondary-, and tertiary-level care settings by:

  ○ Actively assessing patients' level of social connection to identify those who are at increased risk or already experiencing social disconnection and evaluate the level of necessary supports.[305]

  ○ Educating patients about the benefits of social connection and the risk factors for social disconnection as part of primary prevention.

  ○ Leveraging interventions that provide psychosocial support to patients, including involving family or other caregivers in treatment, group therapies, and other evidence-based options.[304]

- **Work with community organizations** to create partnerships that provide support for people who are at risk for, or are struggling with, loneliness, isolation, low social support, or poor-quality relationships.

- Create opportunities for clinicians to partner with researchers to **evaluate the application of evidence-based assessment tools and interventions within clinical settings,** including evaluating the efficacy of applications for specific populations.[10]

What Public Health Professionals and Public Health Departments Can Do

- **Establish social connection as a priority health indicator and social determinant of health** with the goal of improving health and well-being through programs, education, research, and promotion of healthy lifestyles across the lifespan.

- **Develop, lead, and support public education programs, awareness campaigns, and health professional training programs** focused on the health impacts of social disconnection. Integrate social connection as a key component of health promotion and wellness programs focused on related health issues (e.g., suicide, workplace burnout, substance use).[308,309]

- **Study and support research on the causes of social disconnection.**

- **Evaluate, develop, and implement sustainable interventions and strategies** (e.g., programs, campaigns, tools, partnerships) across the social-ecological model to promote greater connection and prevent social disconnection.

- **Consistently and regularly track social connection** using validated metrics (such as the Berkman-Syme Social Network Index, UCLA Loneliness Scale), and validate new measures to capture the full complexity of social connection to guide strategic decision-making, planning, and evaluation of strategies.

Our Epidemic of Loneliness and Isolation: The U.S. Surgeon General's Advisory on the Healing Effects of Social Connection and Community

57

What Researchers and Research Institutions Can Do

- **Establish social connection as a research priority** and support researchers in this field with time, space, and funding.[32]

- **Develop a cross-disciplinary research agenda** including basic, translational, evaluation, and dissemination research that prioritizes systematically mapping outstanding evidence gaps to ensure adequate evidence across all levels of the social-ecological model, sectors of society, and the life course, with attention to inclusion, diversity, equity, access, and modality considerations. This research should include investigations into:

  - The root causes of social disconnection, including how causal mechanisms vary across age, income, culture, race, ethnicity, gender identity, sexual orientation, and health status to advance equity in social well-being for all members of the community, and ensure research is inclusive of under-represented groups.[10,19]

  - What social connection indicators may intersect or act independently, additively, or synergistically to influence risk and resilience for health and other societal outcomes.

  - Fuller examinations of age, developmental, and cohort processes that may influence the onset and progression of disease and other adverse outcomes.

  - Rigorous evaluation of technology's evolving impact on social connection.

  - The effectiveness, efficiency, and acceptability of prevention, intervention, and dissemination approaches.

  - Additional examinations of individual and societal effects of social connection within and beyond health outcomes, including indicators of well-being (e.g., wider community participation, quality of life), prosperity (e.g., educational attainment, employment, economic mobility), and public safety.

- **Develop and establish additional standardized national and local measures** that are regularly evaluated and can be used across basic research, clinical assessment, population surveillance, intervention evaluation, and other contexts.

- **Improve research coordination**, including the development of an accessible evidence database, a way to coordinate utilization of evidence among researchers, and a comprehensive way to track connection and community metrics over time.

What Philanthropy Can Do

- **Fund new programs and invest in existing successful programs** that advance social connection among individuals and within communities, including those that aim to prevent and treat social isolation and loneliness and those that reach populations at highest risk.

- Because social connection can be advanced through programs designed to support other outcomes (e.g., population health, community resilience, public safety, educational attainment, economic progress) funders should **evaluate cross-sector programs for their impact on social connection** by adding social connection and relationship-building as indicators of grantee success.

- **Provide support for adequate evaluation, reporting, and knowledge sharing** about the effectiveness of interventions designed to reduce loneliness and isolation and improve social connection.

- **Convene stakeholders** working to understand or strengthen social connection.

- **Invest in efforts to increase public awareness** and dissemination of findings.

What Schools and Education Departments Can Do

School administrators and leaders, boards of education, boards of trustees, teachers, parent teacher associations, state departments of education, and online learning platforms can all play a role.

- **Develop a strategic plan for school connectedness and social skills with benchmark tracking.** This could include providing regular opportunities and spaces for students to develop social skills and strengthen relationships, and the adoption of evidenced-based practices leveraging elements of the CDC Framework: Whole School, Whole Community, Whole Child.[310] Strategies to enhance connectedness may include promoting quality adult support from family and school staff, peer-led programs, and partnerships with key community groups.

- **Build social connection into health curricula,** including up-to-date, age-appropriate information on the consequences of social connection on physical and mental health, key risk and protective factors, and strategies for increasing social connection.

- **Implement socially based educational techniques** such as cooperative learning projects that can improve educational outcomes as well as peer relations.[311]

- **Create a supportive school environment** that fosters belonging through equitable classroom management, mentoring, and peer support groups that allow students to lean on one another and learn from each other's experiences.

What Workplaces Can Do

- **Make social connection a strategic priority in the workplace** at all levels (administration, management, and employees).[48]

- **Train, resource, and empower leaders and managers** to promote connection in the workplace and implement programs that foster connection. Assess program effectiveness, identify barriers to success, and facilitate continuous quality improvement.

- **Leverage existing leadership and employee training, orientation, and wellness resources** to educate the workforce about the importance of social connection for workplace well-being, health, productivity, performance, retention, and other markers of success.

- **Create practices and a workplace culture** that allow people to connect to one another as whole people, not just as skill sets, and that fosters inclusion and belonging.

- **Put in place policies that protect workers' ability to nurture their relationships outside work** including respecting boundaries between work and non-work time, supporting caregiving responsibilities, and creating a culture of norms and practices that support these policies.

- **Consider the opportunities and challenges posed by flexible work hours and arrangements** (including remote, hybrid, and in-person work), which may impact workers' abilities to connect with others both within and outside of work. Evaluate how these policies can be applied equitably across the workforce.

What Community-Based Organizations Can Do

Community-based organizations include, but are not limited to, membership-based organizations, civic groups, arts and education groups, faith-based organizations, direct service providers, and youth-led organizations. Regardless of whether the mission of a community-based organization is focused on social connection, every organization can promote stronger social connection.

- **Create opportunities and spaces for inclusive social connection** and establish programs that foster positive and safe relationships, including among individuals of different ages, backgrounds, viewpoints, and life experiences.

- **Embed social connection** in internal policies, practices, programs, and evaluations.

- **Actively seek and build partnerships** with other community institutions (schools, health organizations, workplaces) to support those experiencing loneliness and social isolation, and to create a culture of connection in the broader community.

- **Advance public education and awareness efforts** to introduce and elevate the topic of social connection and disconnection among community members.

- **Create and provide education, resources, and support programs** for community members and key populations such as parents, youth, and at-risk populations. These could include community-wide social events, volunteering and community service activities, network-building professional development, and organizational opportunities for involvement by the community.

- **Foster a culture of connection in the broader community** by highlighting examples of healthy social connection and leading by example.

What Technology Companies Can Do

- **Be transparent with data** that illustrates both the positive and negative impacts of technology on social connection by sharing long-term and real-time data with independent researchers to enable a better understanding of technology's impact on individuals and communities, particularly those at higher risk of social disconnection.

- **Support the development and enforcement of industry-wide safety standards** with particular attention to social media, including age-appropriate protections and identity assurance mechanisms, to ensure safe digital environments that enable positive social connection, particularly for minors.

- **Intentionally design technology that fosters healthy dialogue and relationships**, including across diverse communities and perspectives. The designs should prioritize social health and safety as the first principle, from conception to launch to evaluation. This also means avoiding design features and algorithms that drive division, polarization, interpersonal conflict, and contribute to unhealthy perceptions of one's self and one's relationships.

What Media and Entertainment Industries Can Do

- **Create content that models and promotes positive social interactions**, healthy relationships, and reinforces the core values of connection: kindness, respect, service, and commitment to one another.

- **Utilize storylines and narratives** in film, television, and entertainment to provide messages that broaden public awareness of the health benefits of social connection and the risks of social disconnection.

- **Ensure that content related to social connection is scientifically accurate** in collaboration with the scientific community.

- **Avoid content and products that inadvertently increase disconnection or stigma around social disconnection**, recognizing the impact content can have on increasing societal distrust, polarization, and perpetuating harmful stereotypes.

What Parents and Caregivers Can Do

Parents and caregivers play an important role in shaping the experience of social connection. Although focused on parents of young children, many of these recommendations can apply more broadly to all types of caregivers.

- **Invest in your relationship with your child or loved one** by recognizing that strong, secure attachments are protective and a good foundation for other healthy relationships.

- **Model healthy social connection**, including constructive conflict resolution, spending time together, staying in regular contact with extended family, friends, and neighbors, setting time aside for socializing away from technology or social media, and participating in community events.

- **Help children and adolescents develop strong, safe, and stable relationships with supportive adults** like grandparents, teachers, coaches, counselors, and mentors.

- **Encourage healthy social connection with peers** by supporting individual friendships, as well as participation in structured activities such as volunteering, sports, community activities, and mentorship programs.

- **Be attentive to how young people spend their time online.** Delay the age at which children join social media platforms and monitor and decrease screen time in favor of positive, in-person, connection building activities.

- Identify and aim to **reduce behaviors and experiences that may increase the risk for social disconnection**, including bullying and excessive or harmful social media use.

- **Talk to your children about social connection regularly** to understand if they are struggling with loneliness or isolation, to destigmatize talking about these feelings, and to create space for children to share their perspective and needs.

  - Look out for potential warning signs of loneliness and social isolation, such as increases in time spent alone, disproportionate online time, limited interactions with friends, or excessive attention-seeking behavior.[312,313]

  - Connect youth to helpers like counselors, educators, and health care providers if they are struggling with loneliness, isolation, or unhealthy relationships.

What Individuals Can Do

- **Understand the power of social connection and the consequences of social disconnection** by learning how the vital components (structure, function, and quality) can impact your relationships, health, and well-being.

- **Invest time in nurturing your relationships** through consistent, frequent, and high-quality engagement with others. Take time each day to reach out to a friend or family member.

- **Minimize distraction during conversation** to increase the quality of the time you spend with others. For instance, don't check your phone during meals with friends, important conversations, and family time.

- **Seek out opportunities to serve and support others**, either by helping your family, co-workers, friends, or strangers in your community or by participating in community service.

- **Be responsive, supportive, and practice gratitude.**[314,315] As we practice these behaviors, others are more likely to reciprocate, strengthening our social bonds, improving relationship satisfaction, and building social capital.

- **Actively engage with people of different backgrounds and experiences** to expand your understanding of and relationships with others, given the benefits associated with diverse connections.

- **Participate in social and community groups** such as fitness, religious, hobby, professional, and community service organizations to foster a sense of belonging, meaning, and purpose.

- **Reduce practices that lead to feelings of disconnection from others.** These include harmful and excessive social media use, time spent in unhealthy relationships, and disproportionate time in front of screens instead of people.

- **Seek help during times of struggle** with loneliness or isolation by reaching out to a family member, friend, counselor, health care provider, or the 988 crisis line.[316]

- **Be open with your health care provider** about significant social changes in your life, as this may help them understand potential health impacts and guide them to provide recommendations to mitigate health risks.

- **Make time for civic engagement.** This could include being a positive and constructive participant in political discourse and gatherings (e.g., town halls, school board meetings, local government hearings).

- **Reflect the core values of connection** in how you approach others in conversation and through the actions you take. Key questions to ask yourself when considering your interactions with others include: How might kindness change this situation? What would it look like to treat others with respect? How can I be of service? How can I reflect my concern for and commitment to others?

Strengths and Limitations of the Evidence

Hundreds of independent studies across several scientific disciplines have examined the objective physical and mental health outcomes of social connection, social isolation, and loneliness for individuals.[10] Despite the variability in conceptual and methodological approaches used in the research, these findings converge to demonstrate a robust and reliable association between social connection and health outcomes.[37,127,128,317,318]

In addition to significant evidence of correlations between social connection and health, evidence supports a potential causal association. Using the Bradford Hill Guidelines,[58,131] as well as some newer studies leveraging causal epidemiology[319-323] and experimental evidence in animals,[324,325] together suggests a likely causal association between social isolation and a variety of poor health outcomes, including death. In humans, experimental evidence and intervention-based studies using randomized controlled trials also supports the likelihood of a causal association between broader social connection and better health and longer life expectancy.[304]

Importantly, there is evidence of a dose-response relationship between social connection and health.[59] This means that incremental increases in social connection correspond to decreases in risk to health, and conversely, decreases in social connection correspond to increases in risk. Evidence demonstrates this dose-response relationship exists for developmental stages across the lifespan, suggesting that social connection is a continuum from risk (when low) to protection (when high). This suggests social connection is relevant to all humans regardless of our individual positions along the risk trajectory.

Despite the strength of the evidence linking social connection to various health outcomes, certain gaps and limitations in research still exist. For example, few studies examine more than one social connection component (structural, functional, and quality indicators) in the same sample to disentangle the independent, additive, and synergistic effects. This complicates the measurement of an individual's risk associated with lack of social connection (e.g., social isolation, loneliness, social negativity) and confounds the understanding of the unique and complex pathways by which social connection influences health. Further, despite significant changes in the way in which we interact socially, many research studies do not distinguish remote or technology-mediated social connection from traditional means of connecting socially to determine equivalencies and to discern the influence on long-term health and mortality risk. Yet, despite these challenges, the extensive and replicated body of existing evidence offers a compelling basis for elevating the discourse on promoting social connection and addressing social disconnection with targeted public health policies, initiatives, and actions.

In regard to the study of community-level benefits, significant differences exist in how researchers approach community-level social connection across scientific studies. For instance, variations exist in the indicators researchers use to define and measure social connection. While social cohesion, social capital, belonging, and trust are all indicators of connected communities, many studies examine only one of these concepts and few examine all of these to disentangle their relative influence or relate them directly to loneliness and isolation. Complicating matters, some studies also use different terms to refer to the same concept or use the same term to refer to different concepts. Much of this research is correlative in nature and necessitates further study, including among often underrepresented groups, in order to understand causative factors that produce community-level benefits.

Another layer of complexity is how different each community is along a multitude of dynamics and factors such as policies, customs, cultures, assets, challenges, demographics, and more. This variation means there is no "one-size-fits-all" approach to community connection, and it means that different communities will have different needs and desires. Despite all of these differences and complexities, there is strong evidence that points to social connection as an important factor in strengthening communities and community-level outcomes. While more research is needed, the evidence we do have suggests that enhancing community connection may help us address many important community and societal issues.

Acknowledgments

Our Epidemic of Loneliness and Isolation: The Surgeon General's Advisory on the Healing Effects of Social Connection and Community was prepared by the Office of the Surgeon General with valuable contributions from partners across the U.S. Government and external reviewers, including, but not limited to:

Lead Science Editor
Julianne Holt-Lunstad, PhD
Professor of Psychology and Neuroscience, Brigham Young University, and Director, Social Connections Lab. Scientific Chair and Board Member, Foundation for Social Connection, and Global Initiative on Loneliness and Connection

Copy Editor
Susan Golant, MA
Writer and Editor

Department of Health and Human Services (HHS)
Administration for Children and Families (ACF)
Administration for Community Living (ACL)
Agency for Healthcare Research and Quality (AHRQ)
Centers for Disease Control and Prevention (CDC)
    Office of the Director
    Division of Adolescent and School Health
    Division of Population Health
Centers for Medicare and Medicaid Services (CMS)
Health Resources and Services Administration (HRSA)
Indian Health Service (IHS)
National Institutes of Health (NIH)
Office of the Assistant Secretary for Health (OASH)
Office of the Assistant Secretary for Planning and Evaluation (ASPE)
Office of the General Counsel (OGC)
Substance Abuse and Mental Health Services Administration (SAMHSA)

Our Epidemic of Loneliness and Isolation: The U.S. Surgeon General's Advisory on the Healing Effects of Social Connection and Community

69

Reviewers

The Office of the Surgeon General solicited an independent review of the advisory or selected sections in draft form. Reviewers were selected for their technical expertise, and they provided individually many constructive comments. The below reviewers did not view a final version of the advisory prior to its release, nor were they asked to endorse the conclusions or recommendations. We thank the following individuals for their review of the advisory:

Juan R. Albertorio-Diaz, MA, Statistician, National Center for Health Statistics, Centers for Disease Control and Prevention. Senior Research Advisor, Foundation for Social Connection.

Daniel P. Aldrich, PhD, Co-Director, Global Resilience Institute, and Director, Security and Resilience Studies Program. Professor, Political Science and Public Policy, Northeastern University.

Ursula Bauer, PhD, MPH, Deputy Commissioner for Public Health and Director, Office of Public Health, New York State Department of Health.

Lauren Behsudi, Senior Advisor, Administration for Children and Families.

Andrew Breeden, PhD, Program Chief, Social and Affective Neuroscience Program, Division of Neuroscience and Basic Behavioral Science, National Institute of Mental Health.

Katherine V. Bruss, PsyD, Mental Health Lead, Division of Population Health, National Center for Chronic Disease Prevention and Health Promotion, Centers for Disease Control and Prevention.

Paul Cann, MA, (Cambridge University) OBE, Co-founder, UK Campaign to End Loneliness.

Chia-Chia Chang, MPH, MBA, Coordinator, Office for Total Worker Health® Collaborations and New Opportunity Development, and Co-Coordinator, Healthy Work Design and Well-Being Cross Sector Program, National Institute for Occupational Safety and Health, Centers for Disease Control and Prevention.

Katie Clark, Policy Analyst, Office of Integrated Programs and Office of Network Advancement, Center for Innovation and Partnership, the Administration for Community Living.

Thomas K.M. Cudjoe, MD, MPH, Assistant Professor of Medicine, Department of Medicine, Division of Geriatric Medicine and Gerontology, Johns Hopkins University School of Medicine. Scientific Advisory Council Member, Foundation for Social Connection.

Munmun DeChoudhury, PhD, Associate Professor, School of Interactive Computing, Georgia Institute of Technology.

Dona M. Dmitrovic, MHS, Senior Advisor, Office of Recovery, Substance Abuse and Mental Health Services Administration, U.S. Department of Health and Human Services.

Felton James (Tony) Earls, MD, Professor of Social Medicine, Emeritus, Harvard Medical School. Professor of Human Behavior and Development, Emeritus, Harvard T.H. Chan School of Public Health.

Jesse Ellis, MS, MPA, Prevention Manager, Fairfax County Department of Neighborhood and Community Services, Virginia.

Nicole B. Ellison, PhD, Karl E. Weick Collegiate Professor of Information, School of Information, University of Michigan. Scientific Advisory Council Member, Foundation for Social Connection.

Linda Fried, PhD, Dean, Columbia University Mailman School of Public Health. Director, Robert N. Butler Columbia Aging Center.

Edward Garcia III, MHS-PH, Founder and Board Chair, Foundation for Social Connection. Co-Founder and Board Member, Global Initiative on Loneliness and Connection.

Lori Gerhard, Director of the Office of Integrated Programs, Center for Innovation and Partnership, the Administration for Community Living.

Jonathan Gruber, Strategy Lead - Building, Einhorn Collaborative.

Jonathan Haidt, PhD, Professor of Ethical Leadership, New York University Stern School of Business.

Hahrie Han, PhD, Stavros Niarchos Foundation Professor of Political Science, and Inaugural Director, SNF Agora Institute, Johns Hopkins University.

Debra Houry, MD, MPH, Chief Medical Officer and Deputy Director for Program and Science, Centers for Disease Control and Prevention.

Maggie Jarry, MDiv, MS, Senior Emergency Management Specialist, Substance Abuse and Mental Health Services Administration, U.S. Department of Health and Human Services.

Dilip Jeste, MD, Former Senior Associate Dean for Healthy Aging and Senior Care, University of California, San Diego.

David I. Leitman, PhD, Program Chief, Social Neuroscience and Communication in Adult Psychopathology Program, Translational Research Division, National Institute of Mental Health.

Peter Levine, PhD, Lincoln Filene Professor and Associate Dean, Tisch College of Civic Life, Tufts University.

Erin McDonald, PhD, MPP, Senior Advisor and Lead, Equitable Long-Term Recovery and Resilience Plan, U.S. Department of Health and Human Services, Office of the Assistant Secretary of Health, Office of Disease Prevention and Health Promotion.

Melissa C. Mercado, PhD, MSc, MA, Lead Behavioral Scientist, Youth Violence and Emerging Topics, Division of Violence Prevention, National Center for Injury Prevention and Control, Centers for Disease Control and Prevention.

Christopher Mikton, PhD, Technical lead on social connection, Department of Social Determinants of Health, World Health Organization.

Kathleen Mullan Harris, PhD, James E. Haar Distinguished Professor of Sociology, Fellow, Carolina Population Center, University of North Carolina at Chapel Hill.

Phyllis Holditch Niolon, PhD, Senior Scientist for Preventing Adverse Childhood Experiences, Division of Violence Prevention, National Center for Injury Prevention and Control, Centers for Disease Control and Prevention.

Yolanda Ogbolu, PhD, CRNP, FNAP, FAAN, Associate Professor, tenured, Department Chair, Partnerships, Professional Education and Practice, Co-Director Center for Health Equity and Outcomes Research, University of Maryland Baltimore.

Anthony D. Ong, PhD, Professor of Psychology, Cornell University. Professor of Gerontology in Medicine, Weill Cornel Medicine.

Matthew S. Pantell, MD, MS, Assistant Professor, Division of Pediatric Hospital Medicine, Department of Pediatrics, Center for Health and Community, University of California, San Francisco. Scientific Advisory Council Member, Foundation for Social Connection.

Carla M. Perissinotto, MD, MHS, Professor of Medicine, Geriatrics, University of California, San Francisco. Scientific Advisory Council Member, Foundation for Social Connection.

Brian A. Primack, MD, PhD, Dean, College of Public Health and Human Sciences, Oregon State University.

Robert D. Putnam, PhD, Emeritus Professor, Harvard Kennedy School.

Jillian Racoosin, MPH, Executive Director, Foundation for Social Connection.

Harry T. Reis, PhD, Dean's Professor in Arts, Sciences, and Engineering, and Professor of Psychology, University of Rochester. Scientific Advisory Council Member, Foundation for Social Connection.

Joshua Seidman, PhD, Chief Research and Knowledge Officer, Fountain House.

Christine Sinsky, MD, MACP, Vice President, Professional Satisfaction, American Medical Association.

Matthew Lee Smith, PhD, MPH, School of Public Health, Texas A&M University. Scientific Advisory Council Member, Foundation for Social Connection.

Andrew Steptoe, DSc, Professor of Psychology and Epidemiology, University College London, London, UK.

Deb Stone, ScD, MSW, MPH, Lead Behavioral Scientist, Suicide Prevention Team, National Center for Injury Prevention and Control, Centers for Disease Control and Prevention.

Craig W. Thomas, PhD, Director, Division of Population Health, National Center for Chronic Disease Prevention and Health Promotion, Centers for Disease Control and Prevention.

Bert N. Uchino, PhD, Professor, Department of Psychology and Health Psychology Program, University of Utah.

Mark J. Van Ryzin, PhD, Research Associate Professor, University of Oregon. Scientific Advisory Council Member, Foundation for Social Connection.

Laura E. Welder, DrPH, MPH, Behavioral Scientist, Division of Injury Prevention, National Center for Injury Prevention and Control, Centers for Disease Control and Prevention.

Tia Taylor Williams, MPH, CNS, Director, Center for Public Health Policy, Center for School, Health and Education, American Public Health Association.

Our Epidemic of Loneliness and Isolation: The U.S. Surgeon General's Advisory on the Healing Effects of Social Connection and Community

71

References

1. Cigna Corporation. *The Loneliness Epidemic Persists: A Post-Pandemic Look at the State of Loneliness among U.S. Adults.* 2021.

2. Bruce LD, Wu JS, Lustig SL, Russell DW, Nemecek DA. Loneliness in the United States: A 2018 National Panel Survey of Demographic, Structural, Cognitive, and Behavioral Characteristics. *Am J Health Promot.* 2019;33(8):1123-1133.

3. Shovestul B, Han J, Germine L, Dodell-Feder D. Risk factors for loneliness: The high relative importance of age versus other factors. *PLOS ONE.* 2020;15.

4. Holt-Lunstad J, Robles TF, Sbarra DA. Advancing social connection as a public health priority in the United States. *Am Psychol.* 2017;72(6):517-530.

5. Allen KA, Kern ML, Rozek CS, McInereney D, Slavich GM. Belonging: A Review of Conceptual Issues, an Integrative Framework, and Directions for Future Research. *Aust J Psychol.* 2021;73(1):87-102.

6. Sampson RJ, Raudenbush SW, Earls F. Neighborhoods and Violent Crime: A Multilevel Study of Collective Efficacy. *Science.* 1997;277(5328):918-924.

7. Riess H. The Science of Empathy. *Journal of Patient Experience.* 2017;4(2):74-77.

8. Hu T, Zheng X, Huang M. Absence and Presence of Human Interaction: The Relationship Between Loneliness and Empathy. *Frontiers in Psychology.* 2020;11.

9. Prohaska T, Burholt V, Burns A, et al. Consensus statement: loneliness in older adults, the 21st century social determinant of health? *BMJ Open.* 2020;10(8):e034967.

10. National Academies of Sciences Engineering and Medicine (NASEM). *Social Isolation and Loneliness in Older Adults: Opportunities for the Health Care System.* Washington, DC: The National Academies Press; 2020.

11. House BR. How do social norms influence prosocial development? *Current Opinion in Psychology.* 2018;20:87-91.

12. Putnam RD. Bowling Alone: America's Declining Social Capital. In: Crothers L, Lockhart C, eds. *Culture and Politics: A Reader.* New York: Palgrave Macmillan US; 2000:223-234.

13. Moore S, Kawachi I. Twenty years of social capital and health research: a glossary. *J Epidemiol Community Health.* 2017;71(5):513-517.

14. Bourdieu P. The Forms of Capital. In: *Readings in Economic Sociology.* 2002:280-291.

15. National Research Council. *Civic Engagement and Social Cohesion: Measuring Dimensions of Social Capital to Inform Policy.* Washington, DC: The National Academies Press; 2014.

16. Kawachi I, Berkman L. Social Cohesion, Social Capital, and Health. In: Berkman L, Kawachi I, Glymour M, eds. *Social Epidemiology.* Second ed. New York City: Oxford University Press; 2014:174-190.

17. Ehsan A, Klaas HS, Bastianen A, Spini D. Social capital and health: A systematic review of systematic reviews. *SSM - Population Health.* 2019;8:100425.

18. Office of Disease Prevention and Health Promotion, Office of the Assistant Secretary for Health. Social Cohesion. Office of the Secretary, U.S. Department of Health and Human Services. https://health.gov/healthypeople/priority-areas/social-determinants-health/literature-summaries/social-cohesion. Published 2023. Accessed April 2023.

19. Badcock JC, Holt-Lunstad J, Bombaci P, Garcia E, Lim MH. *Position statement: addressing social isolation and loneliness and the power of human connection.* Global Initiative on Loneliness and Connection (GILC).2022.

20. Holt-Lunstad J. Why Social Relationships Are Important for Physical Health: A Systems Approach to Understanding and Modifying Risk and Protection. *Annu Rev Psychol.* 2018;69:437-458.

21. Holt-Lunstad J, Steptoe A. Social isolation: An underappreciated determinant of physical health. *Curr Opin Psychol.* 2021;43:232-237.

22. Brooks KP, Dunkel Schetter C. Social negativity and health: Conceptual and measurement issues. *Social and Personality Psychology Compass.* 2011;5(11):904-918.

23. Berkman LF, Glass T, Brissette I, Seeman TE. From social integration to health: Durkheim in the new millennium. *Social Science & Medicine.* 2000;51(6):843-857.

24. Legros S, Cislaghi B. Mapping the Social-Norms Literature: An Overview of Reviews. *Perspectives on Psychological Science.* 2020;15(1):62-80.

25. Reid AE, Cialdini RB, Aiken LS. Social norms and health behavior. In: *Handbook of behavioral medicine.* Springer; 2010:263-274.

26. Piškur B, Daniëls R, Jongmans MJ, et al. Participation and social participation: are they distinct concepts? *Clinical Rehabilitation.* 2013;28(3):211-220.

27. Levasseur M, Richard L, Gauvin L, Raymond A. Inventory and analysis of definitions of social participation found in the aging literature: Proposed taxonomy of social activities. *Social Science & Medicine.* 2010;71(12):2141-2149.

28. Cohen S, Wills TA. Stress, social support, and the buffering hypothesis. *Psychological Bulletin.* 1985;98:310-357.

29. Spadaro G, Gangl K, Van Prooijen J-W, Van Lange PA, Mosso CO. Enhancing feelings of security: How institutional trust promotes interpersonal trust. *PloS one.* 2020;15(9):e0237934.

30. Rotter JB. A new scale for the measurement of interpersonal trust. *Journal of Personality.* 1967;35:651-665.

31. Gilson L. Trust and the development of health care as a social institution. *Soc Sci Med.* 2003;56(7):1453-1468.

32. Holt-Lunstad J. Social Connection as a Public Health Issue: The Evidence and a Systemic Framework for Prioritizing the "Social" in Social Determinants of Health. *Annual Review of Public Health.* 2022;43(1):193-213.

33. John S. and James L. Knight Foundation, Gallup Inc. *Knight Soul of the Community 2010.* 2010.

34. Aldrich DP, Meyer MA. Social capital and community resilience. *American behavioral scientist.* 2015;59(2):254-269.

35. Aldrich, Daniel. (2012). Building Resilience: Social Capital in Post-Disaster Recovery. 10.7208/chicago/9780226012896.001.0001.

Our Epidemic of Loneliness and Isolation: The U.S. Surgeon General's Advisory on the Healing Effects of Social Connection and Community

72

36. United States Department of Health and Human Services. *Community health and economic prosperity: Engaging businesses as stewards and stakeholders – A report of the Surgeon General.* Atlanta, GA: U.S. Department of Health and Human Services, Centers for Disease Control and Prevention, Office of the Associate Director for Policy and Strategy; 2021.

37. Holt-Lunstad J, Smith TB, Baker M, Harris T, Stephenson D. Loneliness and social isolation as risk factors for mortality: a meta-analytic review. *Perspect Psychol Sci.* 2015;10(2):227-237.

38. Valtorta NK, Kanaan M, Gilbody S, Ronzi S, Hanratty B. Loneliness and social isolation as risk factors for coronary heart disease and stroke: systematic review and meta-analysis of longitudinal observational studies. *Heart.* 2016;102(13):1009-1016.

39. Mann F, Wang J, Pearce E, et al. Loneliness and the onset of new mental health problems in the general population. *Soc Psychiatry Psychiatr Epidemiol.* 2022;57(11):2161-2178.

40. Penninkilampi R, Casey AN, Singh MF, Brodaty H. The Association between Social Engagement, Loneliness, and Risk of Dementia: A Systematic Review and Meta-Analysis. *J Alzheimers Dis.* 2018;66(4):1619-1633.

41. Lazzari C, Rabottini M. COVID-19, loneliness, social isolation and risk of dementia in older people: a systematic review and meta-analysis of the relevant literature. *Int J Psychiatry Clin Pract.* 2021:1-12.

42. Cohen S. Psychosocial Vulnerabilities to Upper Respiratory Infectious Illness: Implications for Susceptibility to Coronavirus Disease 2019 (COVID-19). *Perspect Psychol Sci.* 2020:1745691620942516.

43. Flowers L, Houser A, Noel-Miller C, et al. *Medicare Spends More on Socially Isolated Older Americans.* Washington, D.C.: AARP Public Policy Institute; 2017.

44. Guay F, Boivin M, Hodges EVE. Predicting change in academic achievement: A model of peer experiences and self-system processes. *Journal of Educational Psychology.* 1999;91:105-115.

45. Maher BM, Hynes H, Sweeney C, et al. Medical School Attrition-Beyond the Statistics A Ten Year Retrospective Study. *BMC Medical Education.* 2013;13(1):13.

46. Bowers A, Wu J, Lustig S, Nemecek D. Loneliness influences avoidable absenteeism and turnover intention reported by adult workers in the United States. *Journal of Organizational Effectiveness: People and Performance.* 2022;9(2):312-335.

47. Ozcelik H, Barsade SG. No Employee an Island: Workplace Loneliness and Job Performance. *Academy of Management Journal.* 2018;61(6):2343-2366.

48. United States Department of Health and Human Services. *The U.S. Surgeon General's Framework for Workplace Mental Health and Well-being.* Washington, D.C.: U.S. Department of Health and Human Services, Office of the U.S. Surgeon General; 2022.

49. Morenoff J, Sampson R, Raudenbush S. Neighborhood Inequality, Collective Efficacy, and the Spatial Dynamics of Urban Violence *Criminology.* 2001;39(3):517-558.

50. Kim M, Cho M. Examining the role of sense of community: Linking local government public relationships and community-building. *Public Relations Review.* 2019.

51. Tomova L, Tye K, Saxe R. The neuroscience of unmet social needs. *Soc Neurosci.* 2021;16(3):221-231.

52. Coan JA, Sbarra DA. Social Baseline Theory: The Social Regulation of Risk and Effort. *Curr Opin Psychol.* 2015;1:87-91.

53. Gallup Inc., Meta. *The State of Social Connections.* Washington D.C.: Gallup Inc.,; 2022.

54. Office on Smoking and Health National Center for Chronic Disease Prevention and Health Promotion. Current Cigarette Smoking Among Adults in the United States. https://www.cdc.gov/tobacco/data_statistics/fact_sheets/adult_data/cig_smoking/index.htm#:~:text=Cigarette%20smoking%20remains%20the%20leading,about%201%20in%205%20deaths.&text=In%202020%2C%20nearly%2013%20of,12.5%25)%20currently*%20smoked%20cigarettes. Published 2022. Accessed April 2023.

55. Centers for Disease Control and Prevention. Prevalence of Both Diagnosed and Undiagnosed Diabetes. Centers for Disease Control and Prevention. https://www.cdc.gov/diabetes/data/statistics-report/diagnosed-undiagnosed-diabetes.html. Published 2022. Accessed April 2023.

56. Division of Nutrition Physical Activity and Obesity, National Center for Chronic Disease Prevention and Health Promotion. Adult Obesity Facts. Centers for Disease Control and Prevention. https://www.cdc.gov/obesity/data/adult.html. Published 2022. Accessed April 2023.

57. DiJulio B, Hamel L, Muñana C, Brodie M. *Loneliness and Social Isolation in the United States, the United Kingdom, and Japan: An International Survey.* 2018.

58. Holt-Lunstad J. The Major Health Implications of Social Connection. *Current Directions in Psychological Science.* 2021;30(3):251-259.

59. Yang YC, Boen C, Gerken K, Li T, Schorpp K, Harris KM. Social relationships and physiological determinants of longevity across the human life span. *Proc Natl Acad Sci U S A.* 2016;113(3):578-583.

60. Cacioppo JT, Cacioppo S, Boomsma DI. Evolutionary mechanisms for loneliness. *Cognition & emotion.* 2014;28(1):3-21.

61. Coplan RJ, Bowker JC, Nelson LJ. *The handbook of solitude: Psychological perspectives on social isolation, social withdrawal, and being alone.* John Wiley & Sons; 2021.

62. Steptoe A, Shankar A, Demakakos P, Wardle J. Social isolation, loneliness, and all-cause mortality in older men and women. *Proc Natl Acad Sci U S A.* 2013;110(15):5797-5801.

63. Stokes AC, Xie W, Lundberg DJ, Glei DA, Weinstein MA. Loneliness, social isolation, and all-cause mortality in the United States. *SSM-mental health.* 2021;1:100014.

64. Kannan V, Veazie P. US trends in social isolation, social engagement, and companionship—nationally and by age, sex, race/ethnicity, family income, and work hours, 2003–2020. *SSM - Population Health.* 2023;Volume 21.

65. Putnam RD. *The Upswing: How America Came Together a Century Ago and How We Can Do It Again.*: Simon & Schuster; 2020.

Our Epidemic of Loneliness and Isolation: The U.S. Surgeon General's Advisory on the Healing Effects of Social Connection and Community

73

66. Davern M, Bautista R, Freese J, Morgan S, Smith T. General Social Surveys, 1972-2021 Cross-section [machine-readable data file, 68,846 cases]. In: NORC at the University of Chicago, ed. Chicago: NORC at the University of Chicago,.

67. Pew Research Center. *Political Polarization in the American Public.* 2014.

68. Cox D. *The State of American Friendship: Change, Challenges, and Loss.* Survey Center on American Life; 2021.

69. Kovacs B, Caplan N, Grob S, King M. Social Networks and Loneliness During the COVID-19 Pandemic. *Socius.* 2021;7:2378023120985254.

70. Census Bureau Releases New Estimates on America's Families and Living Arrangements [reports]. United States Census Bureau 2022.

71. Atwell M, Stillerman B, Bridgeland JM. *Health Index 2021: Citizenship During Crisis.* Civic, National Conference on Citizenship, University of Virginia's Miller Center, Democracy Initiative and the Partnership for American Democracy; 2021.

72. Parker K, Horowitz J, Brown A, Fry R, Cohn D, Igielnik R. *What Unites and Divides Urban, Suburban and Rural Communities.* Pew Research Center; 2018.

73. Pew Research Center. *America's Changing Religious Landscape.* Pew Research Center; 2015.

74. Hout M, Smith TW. Fewer Americans Affiliate with Organized Religions, Belief and Practice Unchanged. In:2015.

75. Jones JM. US church membership falls below majority for first time. *Gallup News.* 2021.

76. Putnam RD, Campbell DE. *American Grace: How Religion Divides and Unites Us.* Simon & Schuster; 2010.

77. VanderWeele TJ. Religious communities and human flourishing. *Current Directions in Psychological Science.* 2017;26:476-481.

78. Koenig H, Koenig HG, King D, Carson VB. *Handbook of religion and health.* Oup Usa; 2012.

79. Office of Disease Prevention and Health Promotion. Social Determinants of Health. U.S. Department of Health and Human Services. Healthy People 2030 Web site. https://health.gov/healthypeople/objectives-and-data/social-determinants-health. Published n.d. Accessed April 2023.

80. National Center for Injury Prevention and Control, Division of Violence Prevention. The Social-Ecological Model: A Framework for Prevention. Centers for Disease Control and Prevention. https://www.cdc.gov/violenceprevention/about/social-ecologicalmodel.html. Published 2022. Accessed April 2023.

81. Henry D, Gorman-Smith D, Schoeny M, Tolan P. "Neighborhood matters": Assessment of neighborhood social processes. *American Journal of Community Psychology.* 2014;54:187-204.

82. Lenzi M, Vieno A, Santinello M, Perkins DD. How neighborhood structural and institutional features can shape neighborhood social connectedness: a multilevel study of adolescent perceptions. *Am J Community Psychol.* 2013;51(3-4):451-467.

83. O'Sullivan R, Burns A, Leavey G, et al. Impact of the COVID-19 Pandemic on Loneliness and Social Isolation: A Multi-Country Study. *International Journal of Environmental Research and Public Health.* 2021;18(19):9982.

84. Buecker S, Mund M, Chwastek S, Sostmann M, Luhmann M. Is loneliness in emerging adults increasing over time? A preregistered cross-temporal meta-analysis and systematic review. *Psychological Bulletin.* 2021;147(8):787.

85. Pew Research Center. *Internet/Broadband Fact Sheet.* 2021.

86. Roser M, Ritchie H, Ortiz-Ospin E. Internet. *Our World in Data.* 2015.

87. Perrin M, Atske S. *About three-in-ten U.S. adults say they are 'almost constantly' online.* Pew Research Center; 2021.

88. Vogels E, Gelles-Watnick R, Massarat N. *Teens, Social Media and Technology 2022.* Pew Research Center; 2022.

89. Ortiz-Ospina E. The rise of social media. *Our World in Data.* 2019.

90. Perrin A, Atske S. *Americans with disabilities less likely than those without to own some digital devices.* Pew Research Center; 2021.

91. Vogels E. *Digital divide persists even as Americans with lower incomes make gains in tech adoption.* Pew Research Center; 2021.

92. Vogels E. *Some digital divides persist between rural, urban and suburban America.* Pew Research Center; 2021.

93. Liu D, Ainsworth SE, Baumeister RF. A meta-analysis of social networking online and social capital. *Review of General Psychology.* 2016;20(4):369-391.

94. Domahidi E. The associations between online media use and users' perceived social resources: A meta-analysis. *Journal of Computer-Mediated Communication.* 2018;23(4):181-200.

95. Liu D, Wright KB, Hu B. A meta-analysis of Social Network Site use and social support. *Computers & Education.* 2018;127:201-213.

96. Hancock J, Liu SX, Luo M, Mieczkowski H. Psychological Well-Being and Social Media Use: A Meta-Analysis of Associations between Social Media Use and Depression, Anxiety, Loneliness, Eudaimonic, Hedonic and Social Well-Being. *Anxiety, Loneliness, Eudaimonic, Hedonic and Social Well-Being (March 9, 2022).* 2022.

97. Uhls YT, Ellison NB, Subrahmanyam K. Benefits and costs of social media in adolescence. *Pediatrics.* 2017;140(Supplement_2):S67-S70.

98. Valkenburg PM, Peter J. Online communication among adolescents: An integrated model of its attraction, opportunities, and risks. *Journal of adolescent health.* 2011;48(2):121-127.

99. Yau JC, Reich SM. Are the qualities of adolescents' offline friendships present in digital interactions? *Adolescent Research Review.* 2018;3(3):339-355.

100. Taylor SH, Zhao P, Bazarova NN. Social media and close relationships: a puzzle of connection and disconnection. *Current Opinion in Psychology.* 2021.

101. Ahmad Z, Soroya SH, Mahmood K. Bridging social capital through the use of social networking sites: A systematic literature review. *Journal of Human Behavior in the Social Environment.* 2022:1-17.

102. Noone C, McSharry J, Smalle M, et al. Video calls for reducing social isolation and loneliness in older people: a rapid review. *Cochrane Database Syst Rev.* 2020;5(5):Cd013632.

103. Charalampous M, Grant CA, Tramontano C, Michailidis E. Systematically reviewing remote e-workers' well-being at work: a multidimensional approach. *European Journal of Work and Organizational Psychology.* 2019;28(1):51-73.

104. Griffiths KM, Calear AL, Banfield M. Systematic review on Internet Support Groups (ISGs) and depression (1): Do ISGs reduce depressive symptoms? *J Med Internet Res.* 2009;11(3):e40.

105. Pandya A, Lodha P. Social Connectedness, Excessive Screen Time During COVID-19 and Mental Health: A Review of Current Evidence. *Frontiers in Human Dynamics.* 2021;3.

106. Sen K, Prybutok G, Prybutok V. The use of digital technology for social wellbeing reduces social isolation in older adults: A systematic review. *SSM - Population Health.* 2022;17:101020.

107. Park PS, Blumenstock JE, Macy MW. The strength of long-range ties in population-scale social networks. *Science.* 2018;362(6421):1410-1413.

108. Duplaga M, Szulc K. The Association of Internet Use with Wellbeing, Mental Health and Health Behaviours of Persons with Disabilities. *Int J Environ Res Public Health.* 2019;16(18).

109. Hunt MG, Marx R, Lipson C, Young J. No More FOMO: Limiting Social Media Decreases Loneliness and Depression. *Journal of Social and Clinical Psychology.* 2018;37(10):751-768.

110. Duke É, Montag C. Smartphone addiction, daily interruptions and self-reported productivity. *Addictive Behaviors Reports.* 2017;6:90-95.

111. Dwyer RJ, Kushlev K, Dunn EW. Smartphone use undermines enjoyment of face-to-face social interactions. *Journal of Experimental Social Psychology.* 2018;78:233-239.

112. Kushlev K, Dunn EW. Smartphones distract parents from cultivating feelings of connection when spending time with their children. *Journal of Social and Personal Relationships.* 2018;36(6):1619-1639.

113. Misra S, Cheng L, Genevie J, Yuan M. The iPhone Effect: The Quality of In-Person Social Interactions in the Presence of Mobile Devices. *Environment and Behavior.* 2014;48(2):275-298.

114. Primack BA, Shensa A, Sidani JE, et al. Social Media Use and Perceived Social Isolation Among Young Adults in the U.S. *Am J Prev Med.* 2017;53(1):1-8.

115. Nixon CL. Current perspectives: the impact of cyberbullying on adolescent health. *Adolesc Health Med Ther.* 2014;5:143-158.

116. Chokshi DA. Vicious and Virtuous Cycles in Health. *JAMA Health Forum.* 2023;4(2):e230505.

117. Wang J, Mann F, Lloyd-Evans B, Ma R, Johnson S. Associations between loneliness and perceived social support and outcomes of mental health problems: a systematic review. *BMC Psychiatry.* 2018;18(1):156.

118. Yu G, Sessions JG, Fu Y, Wall M. A multilevel cross-lagged structural equation analysis for reciprocal relationship between social capital and health. *Social Science & Medicine.* 2015;142:1-8.

119. Saeri AK, Cruwys T, Barlow FK, Stronge S, Sibley CG. Social connectedness improves public mental health: Investigating bidirectional relationships in the New Zealand attitudes and values survey. *Australian & New Zealand Journal of Psychiatry.* 2017;52(4):365-374.

120. Seppala E, Rossomando T, Doty J. Social Connection and Compassion: Important Predictors of Health and Well-Being. *Social Research.* 2013;80.

121. Brown KM, Hoye R, Nicholson M. Self-Esteem, Self-Efficacy, and Social Connectedness as Mediators of the Relationship Between Volunteering and Well-Being. *Journal of Social Service Research.* 2012;38(4):468-483.

122. McClain C, Vogels E, Perrin A, Sechopoulos S, Rainie L. *The Internet and the Pandemic.* Pew Research Center; 2021.

123. AmeriCorps. *Volunteering and Civic Life in America Research Summary.* 2021.

124. Leigh-Hunt N, Bagguley D, Bash K, et al. An overview of systematic reviews on the public health consequences of social isolation and loneliness. *Public Health.* 2017;152:157-171.

125. Shor E, Roelfs DJ. Social contact frequency and all-cause mortality: a meta-analysis and meta-regression. *Social Science & Medicine.* 2015;128:76-86.

126. Pinquart M, Duberstein PR. Associations of social networks with cancer mortality: a meta-analysis. *Crit Rev Oncol Hematol.* 2010;75(2):122-137.

127. Rico-Uribe LA, Caballero FF, Martin-Maria N, Cabello M, Ayuso-Mateos JL, Miret M. Association of loneliness with all-cause mortality: A meta-analysis. *PLoS One.* 2018;13(1):e0190033.

128. Holt-Lunstad J, Smith TB, Layton JB. Social relationships and mortality risk: a meta-analytic review. *PLoS Med.* 2010;7(7):e1000316.

129. Berkman LF, Syme SL. Social networks, host resistance, and mortality: a nine-year follow-up study of Alameda County residents. *Am J Epidemiol.* 1979;109(2):186-204.

130. Pantell M, Rehkopf D, Jutte D, Syme SL, Balmes J, Adler N. Social isolation: a predictor of mortality comparable to traditional clinical risk factors. *Am J Public Health.* 2013;103(11):2056-2062.

131. Howick J, Kelly P, Kelly M. Establishing a causal link between social relationships and health using the Bradford Hill Guidelines. *SSM Popul Health.* 2019;8:100402.

132. Czajkowski SM, Arteaga SS, Burg MM. Social support and cardiovascular disease. In: *Handbook of Cardiovascular Behavioral Medicine.* Springer; 2022:605-630.

133. Cené CW, Beckie TM, Sims M, et al. Effects of Objective and Perceived Social Isolation on Cardiovascular and Brain Health: A Scientific Statement From the American Heart Association. *Journal of the American Heart Association.* 2022;11(16):e026493.

134. Caspi A, Harrington H, Moffitt TE, Milne BJ, Poulton R. Socially Isolated Children 20 Years Later: Risk of Cardiovascular Disease. *Archives of Pediatrics & Adolescent Medicine.* 2006;160(8):805-811.

Our Epidemic of Loneliness and Isolation: The U.S. Surgeon General's Advisory on the Healing Effects of Social Connection and Community

75

135. Danese A, Moffitt TE, Harrington H, et al. Adverse childhood experiences and adult risk factors for age-related disease: depression, inflammation, and clustering of metabolic risk markers. *Arch Pediatr Adolesc Med.* 2009;163(12):1135-1143.

136. Manemann SM, Chamberlain AM, Roger VL, et al. Perceived Social Isolation and Outcomes in Patients With Heart Failure. *J Am Heart Assoc.* 2018;7(11).

137. Gorji MH, Fatahian A, Farsavian A. The impact of perceived and objective social isolation on hospital readmission in patients with heart failure: a systematic review and meta-analysis of observational studies. *General Hospital Psychiatry.* 2019;60:27-36.

138. Smith RW, Barnes I, Green J, Reeves GK, Beral V, Floud S. Social isolation and risk of heart disease and stroke: analysis of two large UK prospective studies. *Lancet Public Health.* 2021;6(4):e232-e239.

139. National Center for Chronic Disease Prevention and Health Promotion. Heart Disease and Stroke. Centers for Disease Control and Prevention,. https://www.cdc.gov/chronicdisease/resources/publications/factsheets/heart-disease-stroke.htm. Published 2022. Accessed April 2023.

140. Harding BN, Hawley CN, Kalinowski J, et al. Relationship between social support and incident hypertension in the Jackson Heart Study: a cohort study. *BMJ Open.* 2022;12(3):e054812.

141. National Center for Chronic Disease Prevention and Health Promotion, Division for Heart Disease and Stroke Prevention. High Blood Pressure Symptoms and Causes. Centers for Disease Control and Prevention https://www.cdc.gov/bloodpressure/about.htm. Published 2021. Accessed April 2023.

142. Cornwell EY, Waite LJ. Social network resources and management of hypertension. *J Health Soc Behav.* 2012;53(2):215-231.

143. Ueno T, Nakagomi A, Tsuji T, Kondo K. Association between social participation and hypertension control among older people with self-reported hypertension in Japanese communities. *Hypertension Research.* 2022;45:1-6.

144. Magrin ME, D'Addario M, Greco A, et al. Social support and adherence to treatment in hypertensive patients: a meta-analysis. *Ann Behav Med.* 2015;49(3):307-318.

145. Shahin W, Kennedy GA, Stupans I. The association between social support and medication adherence in patients with hypertension: A systematic review. *Pharm Pract (Granada).* 2021;19(2):2300.

146. Pan J, Hu B, Wu L, Li Y. The Effect of Social Support on Treatment Adherence in Hypertension in China. *Patient Prefer Adherence.* 2021;15:1953-1961.

147. de Wit M, Trief PM, Huber JW, Willaing I. State of the art: understanding and integration of the social context in diabetes care. *Diabet Med.* 2020;37(3):473-482.

148. Brinkhues S, Dukers-Muijrers N, Hoebe C, et al. Socially isolated individuals are more prone to have newly diagnosed and prevalent type 2 diabetes mellitus - the Maastricht study. *BMC Public Health.* 2017;17(1):955.

149. Brinkhues S, Dukers-Muijrers N, Hoebe C, et al. Social Network Characteristics Are Associated With Type 2 Diabetes Complications: The Maastricht Study. *Diabetes Care.* 2018;41(8):1654-1662.

150. Altevers J, Lukaschek K, Baumert J, et al. Poor structural social support is associated with an increased risk of Type 2 diabetes mellitus: findings from the MONICA/KORA Augsburg cohort study. *Diabet Med.* 2016;33(1):47-54.

151. Meisinger C, Kandler U, Ladwig KH. Living alone is associated with an increased risk of type 2 diabetes mellitus in men but not women from the general population: the MONICA/KORA Augsburg Cohort Study. *Psychosom Med.* 2009;71(7):784-788.

152. Norberg M, Stenlund H, Lindahl B, Andersson C, Eriksson JW, Weinehall L. Work stress and low emotional support is associated with increased risk of future type 2 diabetes in women. *Diabetes Res Clin Pract.* 2007;76(3):368-377.

153. Strodl E, Kenardy J. Psychosocial and non-psychosocial risk factors for the new diagnosis of diabetes in elderly women. *Diabetes Res Clin Pract.* 2006;74(1):57-65.

154. Lidfeldt J, Nerbrand C, Samsioe G, Agardh CD. Women living alone have an increased risk to develop diabetes, which is explained mainly by lifestyle factors. *Diabetes Care.* 2005;28(10):2531-2536.

155. Kelly CS, Berg CA. Close relationships and diabetes management across the lifespan: The good, the bad, and autonomy. *Journal of Health Psychology.* 2018;26(2):226-237.

156. Wiebe DJ, Helgeson V, Berg CA. The social context of managing diabetes across the life span. *Am Psychol.* 2016;71(7):526-538.

157. Umeh K. Self-rated health and multimorbidity in patients with type 2 diabetes. *J Health Psychol.* 2022;27(7):1659-1678.

158. Song Y, Nam S, Park S, Shin IS, Ku BJ. The Impact of Social Support on Self-care of Patients With Diabetes: What Is the Effect of Diabetes Type? Systematic Review and Meta-analysis. *Diabetes Educ.* 2017;43(4):396-412.

159. Loprinzi PD, Ford MA. Effects of Social Support Network Size on Mortality Risk: Considerations by Diabetes Status. *Diabetes Spectr.* 2018;31(2):189-192.

160. LeRoy AS, Murdock KW, Jaremka LM, Loya A, Fagundes CP. Loneliness predicts self-reported cold symptoms after a viral challenge. *Health Psychol.* 2017;36(5):512-520.

161. Cohen S, Doyle WJ, Skoner DP, Rabin BS, Gwaltney JM, Jr. Social ties and susceptibility to the common cold. *JAMA.* 1997;277(24):1940-1944.

162. Stephen G, Siobhán H, Muldoon OT, Whittaker AC. Social cohesion and loneliness are associated with the antibody response to COVID-19 vaccination. *Brain Behav Immun.* 2022;103:179-185.

163. Akhter-Khan SC, Tao Q, Ang TFA, et al. Associations of loneliness with risk of Alzheimer's disease dementia in the Framingham Heart Study. *Alzheimer's & Dementia.* 2021;17(10):1619-1627.

164. Donovan NJ, Wu Q, Rentz DM, Sperling RA, Marshall GA, Glymour MM. Loneliness, depression and cognitive function in older U.S. adults. *Int J Geriatr Psychiatry.* 2017;32(5):564-573.

Our Epidemic of Loneliness and Isolation: The U.S. Surgeon General's Advisory on the Healing Effects of Social Connection and Community

76

165. Duffner LA, Deckers K, Cadar D, Steptoe A, de Vugt M, Köhler S. The role of cognitive and social leisure activities in dementia risk: assessing longitudinal associations of modifiable and non-modifiable risk factors. *Epidemiol Psychiatr Sci*. 2022;31:e5.

166. Domènech-Abella J, Mundó J, Haro JM, Rubio-Valera M. Anxiety, depression, loneliness and social network in the elderly: Longitudinal associations from The Irish Longitudinal Study on Ageing (TILDA). *J Affect Disord*. 2019;246:82-88.

167. Loades ME, Chatburn E, Higson-Sweeney N, et al. Rapid Systematic Review: The Impact of Social Isolation and Loneliness on the Mental Health of Children and Adolescents in the Context of COVID-19. *Journal of the American Academy of Child & Adolescent Psychiatry*. 2020;59(11):1218-1239.e1213.

168. Choi KW, Stein MB, Nishimi KM, et al. An Exposure-Wide and Mendelian Randomization Approach to Identifying Modifiable Factors for the Prevention of Depression. *Am J Psychiatry*. 2020;177(10):944-954.

169. Van Orden KA, Witte TK, Cukrowicz KC, Braithwaite SR, Selby EA, Joiner TE, Jr. The interpersonal theory of suicide. *Psychol Rev*. 2010;117(2):575-600.

170. Shaw RJ, Cullen B, Graham N, et al. Living alone, loneliness and lack of emotional support as predictors of suicide and self-harm: A nine-year follow up of the UK Biobank cohort. *J Affect Disord*. 2021;279:316-323.

171. Mezuk B, Rock A, Lohman MC, Choi M. Suicide risk in long term care facilities: A systematic review. *International journal of geriatric psychiatry*. 2014;29(12):1198-1211.

172. Du L, Shi HY, Qian Y, et al. Association between social support and suicidal ideation in patients with cancer: A systematic review and meta-analysis. *Eur J Cancer Care (Engl)*. 2021;30(2):e13382.

173. Conwell Y, Van Orden K, Caine ED. Suicide in older adults. *Psychiatr Clin North Am*. 2011;34(2):451-468, ix.

174. King CA, Merchant CR. Social and interpersonal factors relating to adolescent suicidality: a review of the literature. *Arch Suicide Res*. 2008;12(3):181-196.

175. Troya MI, Babatunde O, Polidano K, et al. Self-harm in older adults: systematic review. *Br J Psychiatry*. 2019;214(4):186-200.

176. Brown EG, Gallagher S, Creaven A-M. Loneliness and acute stress reactivity: A systematic review of psychophysiological studies. *Psychophysiology*. 2018;55(5):e13031.

177. Leschak CJ, Eisenberger NI. Two Distinct Immune Pathways Linking Social Relationships With Health: Inflammatory and Antiviral Processes. *Psychosom Med*. 2019;81(8):711-719.

178. DiMatteo MR. Social Support and Patient Adherence to Medical Treatment: A Meta-Analysis. Health Psychology. 2004;23:207-218.

179. Shankar A, McMunn A, Banks J, Steptoe A. Loneliness, social isolation, and behavioral and biological health indicators in older adults. Health Psychology. 2011;30:377-385.

180. Hooker SA, Masters KS, Park CL. A Meaningful Life is a Healthy Life: A Conceptual Model Linking Meaning and Meaning Salience to Health. *Review of General Psychology*. 2018;22(1):11-24.

181. Cacioppo JT, Cacioppo S, Capitanio JP, Cole SW. The neuroendocrinology of social isolation. *Annu Rev Psychol*. 2015;66:733-767.

182. Mattos Dos Santos R. Isolation, social stress, low socioeconomic status and its relationship to immune response in Covid-19 pandemic context. *Brain Behav Immun Health*. 2020;7:100103.

183. Muscatell KA. Social psychoneuroimmunology: Understanding bidirectional links between social experiences and the immune system. *Brain Behav Immun*. 2021;93:1-3.

184. Robles TF. Annual Research Review: Social relationships and the immune system during development. *J Child Psychol Psychiatry*. 2021;62(5):539-559.

185. Donovan M, Mackey CS, Platt GN, et al. Social isolation alters behavior, the gut-immune-brain axis, and neurochemical circuits in male and female prairie voles. *Neurobiology of Stress*. 2020;13:100278.

186. Dill-McFarland KA, Tang Z-Z, Kemis JH, et al. Close social relationships correlate with human gut microbiota composition. *Scientific Reports*. 2019;9(1):703.

187. Guidi J, Lucente M, Sonino N, Fava GA. Allostatic Load and Its Impact on Health: A Systematic Review. *Psychother Psychosom*. 2021;90(1):11-27.

188. Furman D, Campisi J, Verdin E, et al. Chronic inflammation in the etiology of disease across the life span. *Nat Med*. 2019;25(12):1822-1832.

189. Yang YC, Schorpp K, Harris KM. Social support, social strain and inflammation: evidence from a national longitudinal study of U.S. adults. *Soc Sci Med*. 2014;107:124-135.

190. McHugh Power J, Carney S, Hannigan C, et al. Systemic inflammatory markers and sources of social support among older adults in the Memory Research Unit cohort. *J Health Psychol*. 2019;24(3):397-406.

191. Ershler WB, Keller ET. Age-associated increased interleukin-6 gene expression, late-life diseases, and frailty. *Annu Rev Med*. 2000;51:245-270.

192. Fortmann AL, Gallo LC. Social support and nocturnal blood pressure dipping: a systematic review. *Am J Hypertens*. 2013;26(3):302-310.

193. Teoh AN, Hilmert C. Social support as a comfort or an encouragement: A systematic review on the contrasting effects of social support on cardiovascular reactivity. *Br J Health Psychol*. 2018;23(4):1040-1065.

194. Li H, Xia N. The role of oxidative stress in cardiovascular disease caused by social isolation and loneliness. *Redox Biol*. 2020;37:101585.

195. Froemke RC, Young LJ. Oxytocin, Neural Plasticity, and Social Behavior. *Annual Review of Neuroscience*. 2021;44(1):359-381.

196. Hostinar CE. Recent Developments in the Study of Social Relationships, Stress Responses, and Physical Health. *Curr Opin Psychol*. 2015;5:90-95.

Our Epidemic of Loneliness and Isolation: The U.S. Surgeon General's Advisory on the Healing Effects of Social Connection and Community

77

197. Scatliffe N, Casavant S, Vittner D, Cong X. Oxytocin and early parent-infant interactions: A systematic review. *Int J Nurs Sci.* 2019;6(4):445-453.

198. Silver L, Van Kessel P, Huang C, Clancy L, Gubbala S. *What Makes Life Meaningful? Views From 17 Advanced Economies.* Pew Research Center; 2021.

199. Petrova D, Garcia-Retamero R, Catena A. Lonely hearts don't get checked: On the role of social support in screening for cardiovascular risk. *Preventive Medicine.* 2015;81:202-208.

200. Kim ES, Strecher VJ, Ryff CD. Purpose in life and use of preventive health care services. *Proc Natl Acad Sci U S A.* 2014;111(46):16331-16336.

201. Southwick SM, Sippel L, Krystal J, Charney D, Mayes L, Pietrzak R. Why are some individuals more resilient than others: the role of social support. *World Psychiatry.* 2016;15(1):77-79.

202. Kivimäki M, Steptoe A. Effects of stress on the development and progression of cardiovascular disease. *Nature Reviews Cardiology.* 2018;15(4):215-229.

203. Schore AN. The effects of early relational trauma on right brain development, affect regulation, and infant mental health. *Infant Mental Health Journal.* 2001;22(1-2):201-269.

204. Chandola T, Brunner E, Marmot M. Chronic stress at work and the metabolic syndrome: prospective study. *BMJ.* 2006;332(7540):521-525.

205. McEwen BS. Neurobiological and Systemic Effects of Chronic Stress. *Chronic Stress.* 2017;1:2470547017692328.

206. Birmingham WC, Holt-Lunstad J. Social aggravation: Understanding the complex role of social relationships on stress and health-relevant physiology. *Int J Psychophysiol.* 2018;131:13-23.

207. Kent de Grey RG, Uchino BN, Trettevik R, Cronan S, Hogan JN. Social support and sleep: A meta-analysis. *Health Psychol.* 2018;37(8):787-798.

208. Kobayashi LC, Steptoe A. Social Isolation, Loneliness, and Health Behaviors at Older Ages: Longitudinal Cohort Study. *Ann Behav Med.* 2018;52(7):582-593.

209. Schrempft S, Jackowska M, Hamer M, Steptoe A. Associations between social isolation, loneliness, and objective physical activity in older men and women. *BMC Public Health.* 2019;19(1):74.

210. Christakis NA, Fowler JH. Social contagion theory: examining dynamic social networks and human behavior. *Stat Med.* 2013;32(4):556-577.

211. Driscoll SD. Barriers and facilitators to cervical cancer screening in high incidence populations: A synthesis of qualitative evidence. *Women Health.* 2016;56(4):448-467.

212. Miller TA, Dimatteo MR. Importance of family/social support and impact on adherence to diabetic therapy. *Diabetes Metab Syndr Obes.* 2013;6:421-426.

213. Mendonça G, Cheng LA, Mélo EN, de Farias Júnior JC. Physical activity and social support in adolescents: a systematic review. *Health Educ Res.* 2014;29(5):822-839.

214. Macdonald-Wallis K, Jago R, Sterne JAC. Social Network Analysis of Childhood and Youth Physical Activity: A Systematic Review. *American Journal of Preventive Medicine.* 2012;43(6):636-642.

215. Christakis NA, Fowler JH. The Collective Dynamics of Smoking in a Large Social Network. *New England Journal of Medicine.* 2008;358(21):2249-2258.

216. Moore S, Teixeira A, Stewart S. Effect of network social capital on the chances of smoking relapse: a two-year follow-up study of urban-dwelling adults. *Am J Public Health.* 2014;104(12):e72-76.

217. Blok DJ, de Vlas SJ, van Empelen P, van Lenthe FJ. The role of smoking in social networks on smoking cessation and relapse among adults: A longitudinal study. *Prev Med.* 2017;99:105-110.

218. DuBois DL, Portillo N, Rhodes JE, Silverthorn N, Valentine JC. How Effective Are Mentoring Programs for Youth? A Systematic Assessment of the Evidence. *Psychological Science in the Public Interest.* 2011;12(2):57-91.

219. Steiner RJ, Sheremenko G, Lesesne C, Dittus PJ, Sieving RE, Ethier KA. Adolescent Connectedness and Adult Health Outcomes. *Pediatrics.* 2019;144(1).

220. Beal DJ, Cohen RR, Burke MJ, McLendon CL. Cohesion and Performance in Groups: A Meta-Analytic Clarification of Construct Relations. *Journal of Applied Psychology.* 2003;88:989-1004.

221. Tu M, Cheng Z, Liu W. Spotlight on the Effect of Workplace Ostracism on Creativity: A Social Cognitive Perspective. *Frontiers in Psychology.* 2019;10.

222. Kwan HK, Zhang X, Liu J, Lee C. Workplace Ostracism and Employee Creativity: An Integrative Approach Incorporating Pragmatic and Engagement Roles. *Journal of Applied Psychology.* 2018;103:1358–1366.

223. Patel A., Plowman S. The Increasing Importance of a Best Friend at Work. In: *Workplace:* Gallup Inc.,; 2022.

224. Mann A. *Why We Need Best Friends at Work.* Gallup, Inc.; 2018.

225. Velando-Soriano A, Ortega-Campos E, Gómez-Urquiza JL, Ramírez-Baena L, De La Fuente EI, Cañadas-De La Fuente GA. Impact of social support in preventing burnout syndrome in nurses: A systematic review. *Japan Journal of Nursing Science.* 2020;17(1):e12269.

226. White C, Green RA, Ferguson S, et al. The influence of social support and social integration factors on return to work outcomes for individuals with work-related injuries: a systematic review. *Journal of occupational rehabilitation.* 2019;29(3):636-659.

227. Chetty R, Jackson MO, Kuchler T, et al. Social capital I: measurement and associations with economic mobility. *Nature.* 2022;608(7921):108-121.

228. Chetty R, Jackson MO, Kuchler T, et al. Social capital II: determinants of economic connectedness. *Nature.* 2022;608(7921):122-134.

229. Wilson J. Volunteering. *Annual review of sociology.* 2000:215-240.

230. Jastrzab J, Giordono L, Chase A, et al. *Serving Country and Community: A Longitudinal Study of Service in AmeriCorps.* Washington, DC: Corporation for National and Community Service; 2004.

231. Spera C, Ghertner R, Nerino A, DiTommaso A. Out of work? Volunteers Have Higher Odds of Getting Back to Work. *Nonprofit and Voluntary Sector Quarterly*. 2015;44(5):886-907.

232. National Academies of Sciences *Engineering and Medicine (NASEM). Enhancing Community Resilience through Social Capital and Connectedness: Stronger Together!* Washington, DC: The National Academies Press; 2021.

233. Agency for Toxic Substances and Disease Registry. Concepts of Community. U.S. Department of Health and Human Services,. https://www.atsdr.cdc.gov/communityengagement/pce_concepts.html. Published 2015. Accessed April 2023.

234. Abbott S, Freeth D. Social capital and health: starting to make sense of the role of generalized trust and reciprocity. *J Health Psychol*. 2008;13(7):874-883.

235. Putnam RD. *Better Together: Report of the Saguaro Seminar on Civic Engagement in America*. 2000.

236. Fu F, Nowak MA, Christakis NA, Fowler JH. The Evolution of Homophily. *Scientific Reports*. 2012;2(1):845.

237. Szreter S, Woolcock M. Health by association? Social capital, social theory, and the political economy of public health. *Int J Epidemiol*. 2004;33(4):650-667.

238. Poortinga W. Community resilience and health: The role of bonding, bridging, and linking aspects of social capital. *Health & Place*. 2012;18(2):286-295.

239. Assistant Secretary for Planning and Evaluation. How Human Services Programs Can Use Social Capital to Improve Participant Well-Being and Economic Mobility. U.S. Department of Health and Human Services. https://aspe.hhs.gov/topics/human-services/how-human-services-programs-can-use-social-capital-improve-participant-well-being-economic-mobility. Published n.d. Accessed April 2023.

240. Hunt V, Layton, D., Prince, S.,. *Why diversity matters.* McKinsey&Company; 2015.

241. Hyyppä M. *Healthy ties: Social capital, population health and survival*. 2010.

242. Villalonga-Olives E, Wind T, Kawachi I. Social capital interventions in public health: A systematic review. *Social Science & Medicine*. 2018;212:203-218.

243. Gilbert KL, Quinn SC, Goodman RM, Butler J, Wallace J. A meta-analysis of social capital and health: A case for needed research. *Journal of Health Psychology*. 2013;18(11):1385-1399.

244. Office of Disease Prevention and Health Promotion, Office of the Assistant Secretary for Health. Healthy People 2030. Office of the Secretary, U.S. Department of Health and Human Services. https://health.gov/healthypeople/objectives-and-data/browse-objectives/social-and-community-context. Published n.d. Accessed April 2023.

245. My Health My Community. *Social Connection and Health*. 2018.

246. Nieminen T, Harkanen T, Martelin T, Borodulin K, Koskinen S. Social capital and all-cause mortality among Finnish men and women aged 30-79. *Eur J Public Health*. 2015;25(6):972-978.

247. Zoorob MJ, Salemi JL. Bowling alone, dying together: The role of social capital in mitigating the drug overdose epidemic in the United States. *Drug Alcohol Depend*. 2017;173:1-9.

248. Kawachi I, Kennedy BP, Lochner K, Prothrow-Stith D. Social capital, income inequality, and mortality. *Am J Public Health*. 1997;87(9):1491-1498.

249. Brewster A, Lee S, Curry L, Bradley E. Association Between Community Social Capital and Hospital Readmission Rates. *Population Health Management*. 2019;22(1):40-47.

250. Takada S, Gorbach P, Brookmeyer R, Shoptaw S. Associations of social capital resources and experiences of homophobia with HIV transmission risk behavior and HIV care continuum among men who have sex with men in Los Angeles. *AIDS Care*. 2021;33(5):663-674.

251. Anderson B. HIV Stigma and Discrimination Persist, Even in Health Care. *Virtual Mentor*. 2009;11(12):998-1001.

252. Nugraheni R, Murti B, Irawanto ME, Sulaiman ES, Pamungkasari EP. The social capital effect on HIV/AIDS preventive efforts: a meta-analysis. *J Med Life*. 2022;15(10):1212-1217.

253. Ransome Y, Thurber KA, Swen M, Crawford ND, German D, Dean LT. Social capital and HIV/AIDS in the United States: Knowledge, gaps, and future directions. *SSM - Population Health*. 2018;5:73-85.

254. Jung M, Lin L, Viswanath K. Associations between health communication behaviors, neighborhood social capital, vaccine knowledge, and parents' H1N1 vaccination of their children. *Vaccine*. 2013;31(42):4860-4866.

255. Rönnerstrand B. Social capital and immunization against the 2009 A(H1N1) pandemic in the American States. *Public Health*. 2014;128(8):709-715.

256. Rönnerstrand B. Contextual generalized trust and immunization against the 2009 A(H1N1) pandemic in the American states: A multilevel approach. *SSM - Population Health*. 2016;2:632-639.

257. Ferwana I, Varshney LR. Social capital dimensions are differentially associated with COVID-19 vaccinations, masks, and physical distancing. *PLoS One*. 2021;16(12):e0260818.

258. Hasan MZ, Dean LT, Kennedy CE, Ahuja A, Rao KD, Gupta S. Social capital and utilization of immunization service: A multilevel analysis in rural Uttar Pradesh, India. *SSM Popul Health*. 2020;10:100545.

259. Cronin CE, Franz B, Garlington S. Population health partnerships and social capital: Facilitating hospital-community partnerships. *SSM Popul Health*. 2021;13:100739.

260. Saint Onge JM, Brooks JV. The exchange and use of cultural and social capital among community health workers in the United States. *Sociology of Health & Illness*. 2021;43(2):299-315.

261. Bartscher AK, Seitz S, Siegloch S, Slotwinski M, Wehrhöfer N. Social capital and the spread of Covid-19: Insights from European countries. *Journal of Health Economics*. 2021;80:102531.

262. Borgonovi F, Andrieu E. Bowling together by bowling alone: Social capital and Covid-19. *Social science & medicine*. 2020;265:113501.

263. Fraser T, Aldrich DP, Page-Tan C. Bowling alone or distancing together? The role of social capital in excess death rates from COVID19. *Soc Sci Med.* 2021;284:114241.

264. Fraser T, Page-Tan C, Aldrich DP. Social capital's impact on COVID-19 outcomes at local levels. *Scientific Reports.* 2022;12(1):6566.

265. Makridis CA, Wu C. How social capital helps communities weather the COVID-19 pandemic. *PloS one.* 2021;16(1):e0245135.

266. COVID-19 National Preparedness Collaborators. Pandemic preparedness and COVID-19: an exploratory analysis of infection and fatality rates, and contextual factors associated with preparedness in 177 countries, from Jan I, 2020, to Sept 30, 2021. *Lancet.* 2022;399(10334):1489-1512.

267. Equitable Long-Term Recovery and Resilience Interagency Workgroup. Federal Plan for Equitable Long-Term Recovery and Resilience for Social, Behavioral, and Community Health. Washington, D.C.: U.S. Department of Health and Human Services, Office of the Assistant Secretary for Health, U Office of Disease Prevention and Health Promotion; 2022.

268. National Institutes of Standards and Technology. Community Resilience. U.S. Department of Commerce. https://www.nist.gov/community-resilience. Published n.d. Accessed April 2023.

269. Office of the Assistant Secretary for Preparedness and Response. Community Resilience. U.S. Department of Health and Human Services. https://www.phe.gov/Preparedness/planning/abc/Pages/community-resilience.aspx. Published 2015. Accessed April 2023.

270. Losee JE, Webster GD, McCarty C. Social network connections and increased preparation intentions for a disaster. *Journal of Environmental Psychology.* 2022;79:101726.

271. Stuart BA, Taylor EJ. The Effect of Social Connectedness on Crime: Evidence from the Great Migration. *The Review of Economics and Statistics.* 2021;103(1):18-33.

272. Ross CE, Jang SJ. Neighborhood disorder, fear, and mistrust: The buffering role of social ties with neighbors. *American journal of community psychology.* 2000;28(4):401-420.

273. Resnick MD, Ireland M, Borowsky I. Youth violence perpetration: what protects? What predicts? Findings from the National Longitudinal Study of Adolescent Health. *J Adolesc Health.* 2004;35(5):424.e421-410.

274. David-Ferdon C, Vivolo-Kantor AM, Dahlberg LL, Marshall KJ, Rainford N, Hall JE. A comprehensive technical package for the prevention of youth violence and associated risk behaviors. 2016.

275. Riley C, Roy B, Harari N, et al. Preparing for Disaster: a Cross-Sectional Study of Social Connection and Gun Violence. *J Urban Health.* 2017;94(5):619-628.

276. Lanfear CC. Collective efficacy and the built environment. *Criminology.* 2022;60(2):370-396.

277. Lederman, Daniel, Norman Loayza, and Ana Maria Menendez. "Violent crime: does social capital matter?." *Economic Development and Cultural Change* 50.3 (2002): 509-539.

278. Milam AJ, Buggs SA, Furr-Holden CD, Leaf PJ, Bradshaw CP, Webster D. Changes in Attitudes toward Guns and Shootings following Implementation of the Baltimore Safe Streets Intervention. *J Urban Health.* 2016;93(4):609-626.

279. Butts JA, Roman CG, Bostwick L, Porter JR. Cure Violence: A Public Health Model to Reduce Gun Violence. *Annual Review of Public Health.* 2015;36(1):39-53.

280. National Conference on Citizenship (NCOC). *Civic Health and Unemployment: Can Engagement Strengthen the Economy?* 2011.

281. Knight Foundation. Got Love For Your Community? It May Create Economic Growth, Gallup Study Says. https://knightfoundation.org/press/releases/got-love-for-your-community-it-may-create-economic/. Published 2010. Accessed April 2023.

282. Zenou Y. *Social Interactions and Labor Market Outcomes in Cities* Bonn, Germany: The Institute for the Study of Labor; 2008. IFN Working Paper No. 755,.

283. Ballard PJ, Hoyt LT, Pachucki MC. Impacts of Adolescent and Young Adult Civic Engagement on Health and Socioeconomic Status in Adulthood. *Child Development.* 2019;90(4):1138-1154.

284. Warner M. Building Social Capital: The Role of Local Government. *The Journal of Socio-Economics.* 2001;30:187-192.

285. Department for Digital, Culture, Media and Sport. A connected society: A Strategy for tackling loneliness – laying the foundations for change. London, UK: HM Government; 2018.

286. Duke, N. N., Skay, C. L., Pettingell, S. L., & Borowsky, I. W. (2009). From Adolescent Connections to Social Capital: Predictors of Civic Engagement in Young Adulthood. *Journal of Adolescent Health,* 44(2), 161-168.

287. Campbell DE. Social Networks and Political Participation. *Annual Review of Political Science.* 2013;16(1):33-48.

288. Kim Y. Toward an effective government–public relationship: Organization–public relationship based on a synthetic approach to public segmentation. *Public Relations Review.* 2015;41(4):456-460.

289. Ledingham JA. Government-community relationships: extending the relational theory of public relations. *Public Relations Review.* 2001;27:285-295.

290. Everett JA, Faber NS, Crockett M. Preferences and beliefs in ingroup favoritism. *Front Behav Neurosci.* 2015;9:15.

291. Merton RK. Insiders and Outsiders: A Chapter in the Sociology of Knowledge. *American Journal of Sociology.* 1972;78(1):9-47.

292. Villalonga-Olives E, Kawachi I. The dark side of social capital: A systematic review of the negative health effects of social capital. *Soc Sci Med.* 2017;194:105-127.

293. Mccoy J, Press B, Somer M, Tuncel O. *Reducing Pernicious Polarization: A Comparative Historical Analysis of Depolarization* Carnegie Endowment for International Peace; 2022.

294. Kalmoe N, Mason L. Lethal mass partisanship: Prevalence, correlates, & electoral contingencies. National Capital Area Political Science Association American Politics Meeting; 2019.

295. Hampton K, Sessions L, Ja Her E, Rainie L. *Social isolation and new technology.* Pew Research Center; 2009.

296. Mutz DC. Cross-Cutting Social Networks: Testing Democratic Theory in Practice. *The American Political Science Review.* 2002;96(1):111-126.

297. McPherson M, Smith-Lovin L, Brashears ME. Social Isolation in America: Changes in Core Discussion Networks over Two Decades. *American Sociological Review.* 2006;71(3):353-375.

298. Lee B, Bearman P. Political isolation in America. *Network Science.* 2020;8(3):333-355.

299. Green T. Republicans and Democrats alike say it's stressful to talk politics with people who disagree. 2021. https://www.pewresearch.org/fact-tank/2021/11/23/republicans-and-democrats-alike-say-its-stressful-to-talk-politics-with-people-who-disagree/.

300. Pew Research Center, Edelman. *Edelman Trust Barometer Global Report* 2022.

301. Hurlburt H, Argo Ben Itzhak N, Brown R, Livingston L, Owens S. *Building U.S. Resilience to Political Violence: A Globally Informed Framework for Analysis and Action.* New America; 2019.

302. World Health Organization. Social Isolation and Loneliness. World Health Organization. https://www.who.int/teams/social-determinants-of-health/demographic-change-and-healthy-ageing/social-isolation-and-loneliness. Published 2023. Accessed April 2023.

303. Healthy Places by Design, Social Isolation Learning Network. *Socially Connected Communities: Solutions for Social Isolation.* Healthy Places by Design; 2021.

304. Smith TB, Workman C, Andrews C, et al. Effects of psychosocial support interventions on survival in inpatient and outpatient healthcare settings: A meta-analysis of 106 randomized controlled trials. *PLoS Med.* 2021;18(5):e1003595.

305. Holt-Lunstad J, Perissinotto C. Social Isolation and Loneliness as Medical Issues. *New England Journal of Medicine.* 2023;388(3):193-195.

306. National Academies of Sciences Engineering and Medicine (NASEM). *Toward a 21st Century National Data Infrastructure: Mobilizing Information for the Common Good.* Washington, DC: The National Academies Press; 2023.

307. Holt-Lunstad J. National Health Guidelines for Social Connection: What Is the Evidence in Support and What Might the Guidelines Say? *Policy Insights from the Behavioral and Brain Sciences,.* 2023;10:41-50.

308. National Academy of Medicine. *National Plan for Health Workforce Well-Being.* Washington, DC: The National Academies Press; 2022.

309. United States Department of Health and Human Services. *Addressing Health Worker Burnout: The U.S. Surgeon General's Advisory on Building a Thriving Health Workforce.* Washington, D.C.: U.S. Department of Health and Human Services, Office of the U.S. Surgeon General; 2022.

310. Division of Population Health, National Center for Chronic Disease Prevention and Health Promotion. Whole School, Whole Community, Whole Child (WSCC). Centers for Disease Control and Prevention,. https://www.cdc.gov/healthyschools/wscc/index.htm. Published 2023. Accessed April 2023.

311. Roseth CJ, Johnson DW, Johnson RT. Promoting early adolescents' achievement and peer relationships: the effects of cooperative, competitive, and individualistic goal structures. *Psychol Bull.* 2008;134(2):223-246.

312. Mental Health America. Is Your Child Lonely? (For Parents). Mental Health America. https://mhanational.org/your-child-lonely-parents. Published 2023. Accessed April 2023.

313. Ehmke R, Allerhand L, Vibert B. How to Help Kids Who Are Lonely. Child Mind Institute https://childmind.org/article/how-to-help-kids-who-are-lonely/. Published 2022. Accessed April 2023.

314. Canevello A, Crocker J. Creating good relationships: responsiveness, relationship quality, and interpersonal goals. *J Pers Soc Psychol.* 2010;99(1):78-106.

315. Caputo A. The Relationship Between Gratitude and Loneliness: The Potential Benefits of Gratitude for Promoting Social Bonds. *Eur J Psychol.* 2015;11(2):323-334.

316. Substance Abuse and Mental Health Services Administration. 988 Suicide and Crisis Lifeline. Substance Abuse and Mental Health Services Administration,. https://988lifeline.org/. Published n.d. Accessed April 2023.

317. Roelfs DJ, Shor E, Curreli M, Clemow L, Burg MM, Schwartz JE. Widowhood and mortality: a meta-analysis and meta-regression. *Demography.* 2012;49(2):575-606.

318. Roelfs DJ, Shor E, Kalish R, Yogev T. The rising relative risk of mortality for singles: meta-analysis and meta-regression. *Am J Epidemiol.* 2011;174(4):379-389.

319. Fedak KM, Bernal A, Capshaw ZA, Gross S. Applying the Bradford Hill criteria in the 21st century: how data integration has changed causal inference in molecular epidemiology. *Emerging Themes in Epidemiology.* 2015;12(1):14.

320. Cox LA, Jr. Modernizing the Bradford Hill criteria for assessing causal relationships in observational data. *Crit Rev Toxicol.* 2018;48(8):682-712.

321. Peng A, Tang Y, He S, Ji S, Dong B, Chen L. Association between loneliness, sleep behavior and quality: a propensity-score-matched case-control study. *Sleep Med.* 2021;86:19-24.

322. Elovainio M, Hakulinen C, Pulkki-Råback L, et al. Contribution of risk factors to excess mortality in isolated and lonely individuals: an analysis of data from the UK Biobank cohort study. *Lancet Public Health.* 2017;2(6):e260-e266.

323. Zheng C, He MH, Huang JR, He Y. Causal Relationships Between Social Isolation and Osteoarthritis: A Mendelian Randomization Study in European Population. *Int J Gen Med.* 2021;14:6777-6786.

324. Cacioppo JT, Cacioppo S, Cole SW, Capitanio JP, Goossens L, Boomsma DI. Loneliness across phylogeny and a call for comparative studies and animal models. *Perspect Psychol Sci.* 2015;10(2):202-212.

325. Cole SW, Capitanio JP, Chun K, Arevalo JM, Ma J, Cacioppo JT. Myeloid differentiation architecture of leukocyte transcriptome dynamics in perceived social isolation. *Proc Natl Acad Sci U S A.* 2015;112(49):15142-15147.

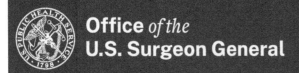

Office *of the*
U.S. Surgeon General